Thicket
nature-inspired cable knits
by Knit Picks

Copyright 2022 © Knit Picks

All rights reserved. This book or any portion thereof may not be reproduced or used in any manner whatsoever without the express written permission of the publisher except for the use of brief quotations in a book review.

Photography by Elizabeth LePage
Graphic Design by Lee Meredith
Creative Direction by Hillary Elliott

Printed in the United States of America
First Printing, 2022

ISBN 978-1-62767-315-0

Versa Press, Inc.

800-447-7829
www.versapress.com

CONTENTS

Brushwood Wrap — 10
by Neisha Abdulla

Grayrigg Pullover — 18
by Bridget Pupillo

Fleville Wrap — 28
by Bérangère Cailliau

Winter Ivy Pullover — 36
by Mari Tobita

Korzina Cowl — 46
by Lisa Ebert

Treeline Sweater — 52
by Camilyn Crane

Raquettes Shawl — 60
by Karen Riehl

Antrim Cardigan — 68
by Jill Wright

Fir Bough Hat — 78
by Emily Kintigh

Roots Jumper — 84
by Helen Metcalfe

Country Crossroads Scarf — 92
by Tina Spencer

Slalom Pullover — 98
by Anni Howard

Deilen Hood — 106
by Christie Wareham-Norfolk

Kinriver — 116
by Amy Snell

Emre Pullover & Cardigan — 126
by Todd Gocken

Glossary — 142

BRUSHWOOD WRAP
by Neisha Abdulla

FINISHED MEASUREMENTS
17.25" width × 91.25" length

YARN
Wool of the Andes™ Tweed (worsted weight, 80% Peruvian Highland Wool, 20% Donegal Tweed; 110 yards/50g): Lost Lake Heather 25447, 14 skeins

NEEDLES
US 6 (4mm) straight or circular needles (24" or longer), or size to obtain gauge

NOTIONS
Yarn Needle
Cable Needle
Spare Needle in gauge size for 3-Needle Bind Off
Blocking Pins and/or Wires

GAUGE
25 sts and 27 rows = 4" in Brushwood Pattern, blocked

For pattern support, contact neisha1@outlook.com

Brushwood Wrap

Notes:
Brushwood is inspired by winter's undergrowth, highlighting the knotted and intertwined plant forms left behind at the end of the season. This gender-neutral design is constructed using a combination of carefully placed cables that mimic twisted, interwoven tendrils.

Brushwood is constructed in two halves and joined together using a 3-Needle Bind Off. The rib at each end leads gently into the cable patterns to give a seamless transition. There is a 2-stitch selvage at the beginning and end of each row.

Chart is worked flat; read RS rows (odd numbers) from right to left, and WS rows (even numbers) from left to right.

2-St Selvage (worked over 2 sts at beginning and end of row)
Row 1 (RS): Sl1 WYIB, K1, work as written to last 2 sts, Sl1 WYIB, P1.
Row 2 (WS): Sl1 WYIB, P1, work as written to last 2 sts, Sl1 WYIF, P1.
Rep Rows 1–2 throughout entire pattern.

Ribbing Pattern (flat over 104 sts)
Row 1 (RS): P4, (K3, P2) two times, K3, P5, K3, P3, K6, P2, K4, P3, (K2, P2) four times, K2, P3, K4, P2, K6, P3, P5, (K3, P2) two times, K3, P4.
Row 2 (WS): K4, (P3, K2) two times, P3, K5, P3, K3, P6, K2, P4, K3, (P2, K2) four times, P2, K3, P4, K2, P6, K3, P3, K5, (P3, K2) two times, P3, K4.
Rep Rows 1–2 for pattern.

3/1 RPC (3 over 1 Right Cable, Purl back)
Sl1 to CN, hold in back; K3, P1 from CN.

3/2 RPC (3 over 2 Right Cable, Purl back)
Sl2 to CN, hold in back; K3, P2 from CN.

3/2 LPC (3 over 2 Left Cable, Purl back)
Sl3 to CN, hold in front; P2, K3 from CN.

3/1 LPC (3 over 1 Left Cable, Purl back)
Sl3 to CN, hold in front; P1, K3 from CN.

3/2 RC (3 over 2 Right Cable)
Sl2 to CN, hold in back; K3, K2 from CN.

3/3 LC (3 over 3 Left Cable)
Sl3 to CN, hold in front; K3, K3 from CN.

3/1 LC (3 over 1 Left Cable)
Sl3 to CN, hold in front; K1, K3 from CN.

3/2 LC (3 over 2 Left Cable)
Sl3 to CN, hold in front; K2, K3 from CN.

3/1 RC (3 over 1 Right Cable)
Sl1 to CN, hold in back; K3, K1 from CN.

3/3 RC (3 over 3 Right Cable)
Sl3 to CN, hold in back; K3, K3 from CN.

Brushwood Pattern (flat over 104 sts)
Row 1: P4, (K3, P2) two times, K3, P5, K3, P3, K6, P2, 3/1 RPC, P3, (K2, P2) four times, K2, P3, 3/1 LPC, P2, K6, P3, K3, P5, (K3, P2) two times, K3, P4.
Row 2: K4, (P3, K2) two times, P3, K5, P3, K3, P6, K2, P3, K4, (P2, K2) four times, P2, K4, P3, K2, P6, K3, P3, K5, (P3, K2) two times, P3, K4.
Row 3: P4, (K3, P2) two times, K3, P5, K3, P3, K6, 3/2 RPC, P4, (3/3 LC, P2) two times, K2, P4, 3/2 LPC, K6, P3, K3, P5, (K3, P2) two times, K3, P4.
Row 4: K4, (P3, K2) two times, P3, K5, P3, K3, P9, K6, (P2, K2) four times, P2, K6, P9, K3, P3, K5, (P3, K2) two times, P3, K4.
Row 5: P4, 3/1 LPC, 3/1 RPC, P2, K3, P5, K3, P3, K4, 3/2 RPC, P6, (K2, P2) four times, K2, P6, 3/2 LPC, K4, P3, K3, P5, K3, P2, 3/1 LPC, 3/1 RPC, P4.
Row 6: K5, P6, K3, P3, K5, P3, K3, P7, K8, (P2, K2) four times, P2, K8, P7, K3, P3, K5, P3, K3, P6, K5.
Row 7: P5, 3/3 LC, P3, K3, P5, K3, P3, 3/1 RPC, P8, (K2, P2) four times, K2, P8, 3/1 LPC, K3, P3, K3, P5, K3, P3, 3/3 RC, P5.
Row 8: K5, P6, K3, P3, K5, P3, K3, P6, K9, (P2, K2) four times, P2, K9, P6, K3, P3, K5, P3, K3, P6, K5.
Row 9: P4, 3/1 RPC, 3/1 LPC, P2, K3, P5, K3, P3, 3/3 LC, P9, K2, (P2, 3/3 RC) two times, P9, 3/3 RC, P3, K3, P5, K3, P2, 3/1 RPC, 3/1 LPC, P4.
Row 10: K4, (P3, K2) two times, P3, K5, P3, K3, P6, K9, (P2, K2) four times, P2, K9, P6, K3, P3, K5, (P3, K2) two times, P3, K4.
Row 11: P4, K3, P2, 3/1 LPC, 3/1 RPC, P5, K3, P3, K3, 3/1 LC, P8, (K2, P2) four times, K2, P8, 3/1 RC, K3, P3, K3, P5, 3/1 LPC, 3/1 RPC, P2, K3, P4.
Row 12: K4, P3, K3, P6, K6, P3, K3, P7, K8, (P2, K2) four times, P2, K8, P7, K3, P3, K6, P6, K3, P3, K4.
Row 13: P4, K3, P3, 3/3 RC, P6, K3, P3, K4, 3/2 LC, P6, (K2, P2) four times, K2, P6, 3/2 RC, K4, P3, K3, P6, 3/3 LC, P3, K3, P4.
Row 14: K4, P3, K3, P6, K6, P3, K3, P9, K6, (P2, K2) four times, P2, K6, P9, K3, P3, K6, P6, K3, P3, K4.
Row 15: P4, K3, P2, 3/1 RPC, 3/1 LPC, P5, K3, P3, K6, 3/2 LPC, P4, (3/3 LC, P2) two times, K2, P4, 3/2 RPC, K6, P3, K3, P5, 3/1 RPC, 3/1 LPC, P2, K3, P4.
Row 16: K4, (P3, K2) two times, P3, K5, P3, K3, P6, K2, P3, K4, (P2, K2) four times, P2, K4, P3, K2, P6, K3, P3, K5, (P3, K2) two times, P3, K4.
Row 17: P4, (K3, P2) two times, K3, P5, K3, P3, K6, P2, 3/1 LPC, P3, (K2, P2) four times, K2, P3, 3/1 RPC, P2, K6, P3, K3, P5, (K3, P2) two times, K3, P4.
Row 18: K4, (P3, K2) two times, P3, K5, P3, K3, P6, K3, P3, K3, (P2, K2) four times, P2, K3, P3, K3, P6, K3, P3, K5, (P3, K2) two times, P3, K4.
Row 19: P4, (K3, P2) two times, K3, P5, 3/1 LPC, P2, K6, P3, K3, P3, (K2, P2) four times, K2, P3, P3, K3, P6, K2, 3/1 RPC, P5, (K3, P2) two times, K3, P4.
Row 20: K4, (P3, K2) two times, P3, K6, P3, K2, P6, K3, P3, K3, (P2, K2) four times, P2, K3, P3, K3, P6, K2, P3, K6, (P3, K2) two times, P3, K4.

Row 21: P4, (K3, P2) two times, K3, P6, 3/2 LPC, K6, P3, K3, P3, K2, (P2, 3/3 RC) two times, P3, K3, P3, K6, 3/2 RPC, P6, (K3, P2) two times, K3, P4.

Row 22: K4, (P3, K2) two times, P3, K8, P9, K3, P3, K3, (P2, K2) four times, P2, K3, P3, K3, P9, K8, (P3, K2) two times, P3, K4.

Row 23: P4, 3/1 LPC, 3/1 RPC, P2, K3, P8, 3/2 LPC, K4, P3, K3, P3, (K2, P2) four times, K2, P3, K3, P3, K4, 3/2 RPC, P8, K3, P2, 3/1 LPC, 3/1 RPC, P4.

Row 24: K5, P6, K3, P3, K10, P7, K3, P3, K3, (P2, K2) four times, P2, K3, P3, K3, P7, K10, P3, K3, P6, K5.

Row 25: P5, 3/3 LC, P3, K3, P10, 3/1 LPC, (K3, P3) two times, (K2, P2) four times, K2, P3, K3, P3, K3, 3/1 RPC, P10, K3, P3, 3/3 RC, P5.

Row 26: K5, P6, K3, P3, K11, P8, K3, P3, K3, (P2, K2) four times, P2, K3, P3, K3, P6, K11, P3, K3, P6, K5.

Row 27: P4, 3/1 RPC, 3/1 LPC, P2, K3, P11, 3/3 RC, P3, K3, P3, (3/3 LC, P2) two times, K2, P3, K3, P3, 3/3 LC, P11, K3, P2, 3/1 RPC, 3/1 LPC, P4.

Row 28: K4, (P3, K2) two times, P3, K11, P6, K3, P3, K3, (P2, K2) four times, P2, K3, P3, K3, P6, K11, (P3, K2) two times, P3, K4.

Row 29: P4, K3, P2, 3/1 LPC, 3/1 RPC, P10, 3/1 RC, (K3, P3) two times, (K2, P2) four times, K2, P3, K3, P3, K3, 3/1 LC, P10, 3/1 LPC, 3/1 RPC, P2, K3, P4.

Row 30: K4, P3, K3, P6, K11, P7, K3, P3, K3, (P2, K2) four times, P2, K3, P3, K3, P7, K11, P6, K3, P3, K4.

Row 31. P4, K3, P3, 3/3 RC, P9, 3/2 RC, K4, P3, K3, P3, (K2, P2) four times, K2, P3, K3, P3, K4, 3/2 LC, P9, 3/3 RC, P3, K3, P4.

Row 32: K4, P3, K3, P6, K9, P9, K3, P3, K3, (P2, K2) four times, P2, K3, P3, K3, P9, K9, P6, K3, P3, K4.

Row 33: P4, K3, P2, 3/1 RPC, 3/1 LPC, P6, 3/2 RPC, K6, P3, K3, P3, K2, (P2, 3/3 RC) two times, P3, K3, P3, K6, 3/2 LPC, P6, 3/1 RPC, 3/1 LPC, P2, K3, P4.

Row 34: K4, (P3, K2) two times, P3, K6, P3, K2, P6, K3, P3, K3, (P2, K2) four times, P2, K3, P3, K3, P6, K2, P3, K6, (P3, K2) two times, P3, K4.

Row 35: P4, (K3, P2) two times, K3, P5, 3/1 RPC, P2, K6, P3, K3, P3, (K2, P2) four times, K2, P3, K3, P3, K6, P2, 3/1 LPC, P5, (K3, P2) two times, K3, P4.

Row 36: K4, (P3, K2) two times, P3, K5, P3, K3, P6, K3, P3, K3, (P2, K2) four times, P2, K3, P3, K3, P6, K3, P3, K5, (P3, K2) two times, P3, K4.

Rep Rows 1–36 for pattern.

DIRECTIONS

Work 2-St Selvage at the beginning and end of each row throughout the pattern.

First Half
Rib
CO 108 sts.
Work Rows 1–2 of Ribbing Pattern ten times.

Body
Work Rows 1–36 of Brushwood Pattern, from chart or written instructions, eight times.

Place work on a spare needle until ready to join halves.

Second Half
Work another piece, the same as the first half.

Join the Two Pieces Together
With RSs tog, join the two halves using 3-Needle Bind Off.

Finishing
Weave in ends, wash, and block to measurements.

Brushwood Pattern, Stitches 52–104

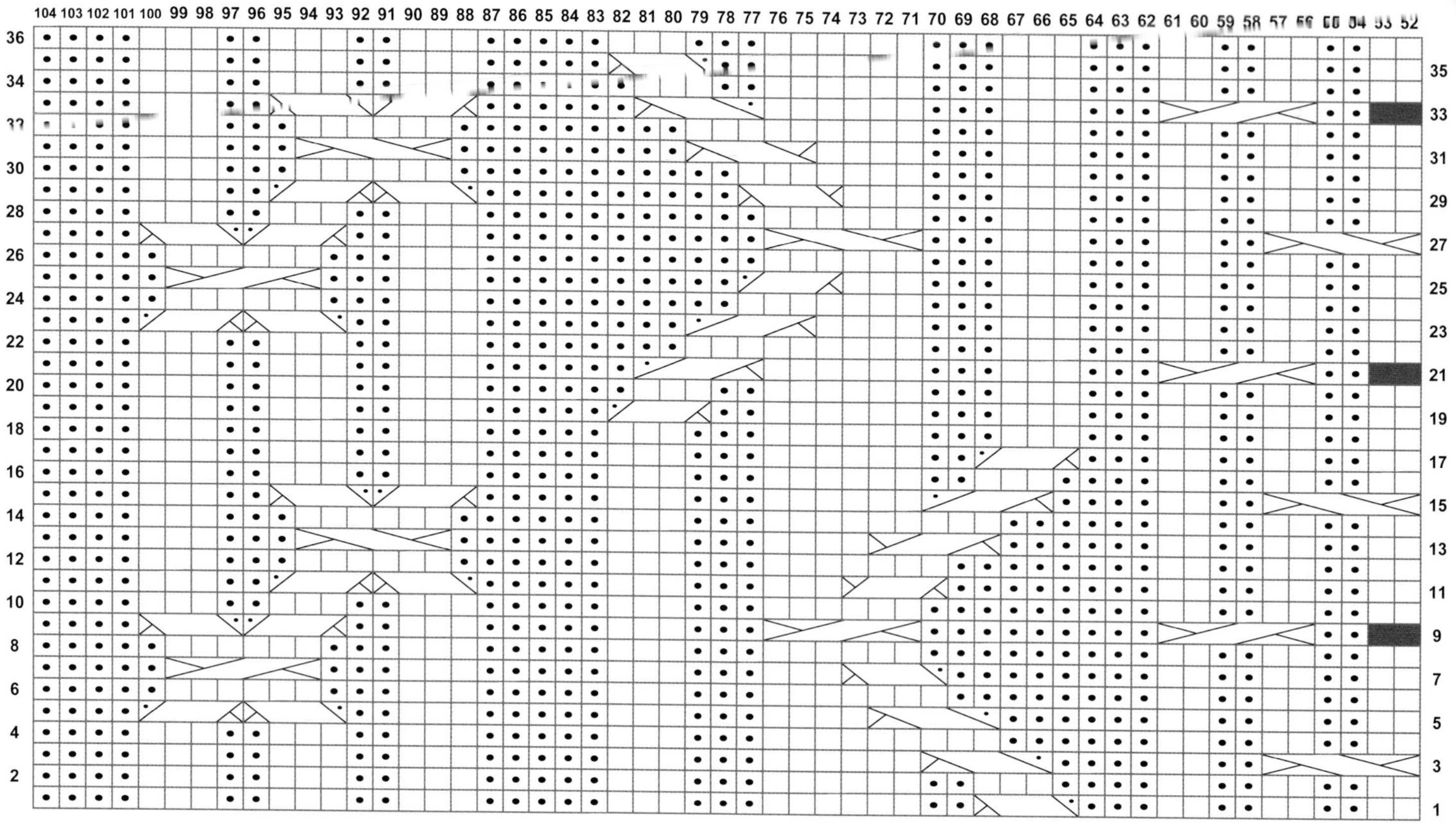

LEGEND

■ **No Stitch**
Placeholder—no stitch made

□ **K**
RS: Knit stitch
WS: Purl stitch

• **P**
RS: Purl stitch
WS: Knit stitch

3 over 1 Right Cable (3/1 RC)
Sl1 to CN, hold in back; K3, K1 from CN

3 over 1 Left Cable (3/1 LC)
Sl3 to CN, hold in front; K1, K3 from CN

3 over 1 Right Cable, Purl back (3/1 RPC)
Sl1 to CN, hold in back; K3, P1 from CN

3 over 1 Left Cable, Purl back (3/1 LPC)
Sl3 to CN, hold in front; P1, K3 from CN

3 over 2 Right Cable (3/2 RC)
Sl2 to CN, hold in back; K3, K2 from CN

3 over 2 Left Cable (3/2 LC)
Sl3 to CN, hold in front; K2, K3 from CN

3 over 2 Right Cable, Purl back (3/2 RPC)
Sl2 to CN, hold in back; K3, P2 from CN

3 over 2 Left Cable, Purl back (3/2 LPC)
Sl3 to CN, hold in front; P2, K3 from CN

3 over 3 Right Cable (3/3 RC)
Sl3 to CN, hold in back; K3, K3 from CN

3 over 3 Left Cable (3/3 LC)
Sl3 to CN, hold in front; K3, K3 from CN

Brushwood Wrap

Brushwood Pattern, Stitches 1–51

GRAYRIGG PULLOVER
by Bridget Pupillo

FINISHED MEASUREMENTS
32 (34, 38, 42)(46, 50, 54)(58, 62)" finished chest measurement; meant to be worn with 4-8" positive ease
Samples are 34" (blue) & 42" (gray); models are 35" except short-haired male model is 38"

YARN
High Desert™ (worsted weight, 100% American Wool; 217 yards/100g): Stargazing 29269 or Quail 29265, 6 (6, 7, 8)(8, 9, 10)(11, 12) skeins

NEEDLES
US 5 (3.75mm) 16" and 32" circular needles and DPNs, or size to obtain gauge

US 4 (3.5mm) 16" and 32" circular needles and DPNs, or one size smaller than size used to obtain gauge

NOTIONS
Yarn Needle
Removable Stitch Markers
Cable Needle or extra DPN
Scrap Yarn or Stitch Holders

GAUGE
20 sts and 30 rnds = 4" in Stockinette Stitch in the round, blocked
30 sts and 32 rnds = 4" in Chart 1 Cable Panel in the round, blocked

For pattern support, contact brigittissima@gmail.com

Grayrigg Pullover

Notes:
Evoking the ancient stones of the Cumbrian countryside, Grayrigg's intertwining cables stand out against a backdrop of simple Stockinette Stitch. This saddle-shoulder pullover features cable panels down the center front and back, with smaller panels along the sleeves.

The Grayrigg Pullover is worked in the round from the bottom up. Sleeves are worked separately and attached to the body while working the yoke. The saddle-shoulder yoke is worked in the round to the neck, and finished off with a simple ribbed neckline.

Chart 1 is worked in the round; read each chart row from right to left as a RS row. Chart 2 is worked both in the round and flat; when working flat, read RS rows (odd numbers) from right to left, and WS rows (even numbers) from left to right.

2/2 LC (2 over 2 Left Cable)
Sl2 to CN, hold in front; K2, K2 from CN.

2/2 RC (2 over 2 Right Cable)
Sl2 to CN, hold in back; K2, K2 from CN.

2/1 LPC (2 over 1 Left Cable, Purl back)
Sl2 to CN, hold in front; P1, K2 from CN.

2/1 RPC (2 over 1 Right Cable, Purl back)
Sl1 to CN, hold in back; K2, P1 from CN.

Chart 1 (in the round over 46 sts)
Rnd 1: P2, (K2, P3, 2/1 RPC, 2/2 LC, 2/1 LPC, P3, K2, P2) two times.
Rnd 2: P2, (K2, P3, K2, P1, K4, P1, K2, P3, K2, P2) two times.
Rnd 3: P2, (K2, P2, 2/1 RPC, P1, K4, P1, 2/1 LPC, P2, K2, P2) two times.
Rnd 4: (P2, K2) two times, P2, K4, (P2, K2) four times, P2, K4, (P2, K2) two times, P2.
Rnd 5: P2, (K2, P1, 2/1 RPC, P2, K4, P2, 2/1 LPC, P1, K2, P2) two times.
Rnd 6: P2, (K2, P1, K2, P3, K4, P3, K2, P1, K2, P2) two times.
Rnd 7: P2, (K2, 2/1 RPC, P3, 2/2 LC, P3, 2/1 LPC, K2, P2) two times.
Rnd 8: P2, *(K4, P4) two times, K4, P2; rep from * once more.
Rnd 9: P2, (2/2 LC, P3, 2/1 RPC, 2/1 LPC, P3, 2/2 LC, P2; rep from * once more.
Rnd 10: P2, (K4, P3, K2, P2, K2, P3, K4, P2) two times.
Rnd 11: P2, (K4, P2, 2/1 RPC, P2, 2/1 LPC, P2, K4, P2) two times.
Rnd 12: P2, (K4, P2, K2, P4, K2, P2, K4, P2) two times.
Rnd 13: P2, (K4, P1, 2/1 RPC, P4, 2/1 LPC, P1, K4, P2) two times.
Rnd 14: P2, (K4, P1, K2, P6, K2, P1, K4, P2) two times.
Rnd 15: P2, (2/2 LC, 2/1 RPC, P6, 2/1 LPC, 2/2 LC, P2) two times.
Rnd 16: P2, (K6, P8, K6, P2) two times.
Rnd 17: P2, (K2, 2/2 RC, P8, 2/2 RC, K2, P2) two times.
Rnd 18: P2, (K6, P8, K6, P2) two times.
Rnd 19: P2, (2/2 LC, 2/1 LPC, P6, 2/1 RPC, 2/2 LC, P2) two times.
Rnd 20: P2, (K4, P1, K2, P6, K2, P1, K4, P2) two times.
Rnd 21: P2, (K4, P1, 2/1 LPC, P4, 2/1 RPC, P1, K4, P2) two times.
Rnd 22: P2, (K4, P2, K2, P4, K2, P2, K4, P2) two times.
Rnd 23: P2, (K4, P2, 2/1 LPC, P2, 2/1 RPC, P2, K4, P2) two times.
Rnd 24: P2, (K4, P3, K2, P2, K2, P3, K4, P2) two times.
Rnd 25: P2, (2/2 LC, P3, 2/1 LPC, 2/1 RPC, P3, 2/2 LC, P2) two times.
Rnd 26: P2, *(K4, P4) two times, K4, P2; rep from * once more.
Rnd 27: P2, (K2, 2/1 LPC, P3, 2/2 LC, P3, 2/1 RPC, K2, P2) two times.
Rnd 28: P2, (K2, P1, K2, P3, K4, P3, K2, P1, K2, P2) two times.
Rnd 29: P2, (K2, P1, 2/1 LPC, P2, K4, P2, 2/1 RPC, P1, K2, P2) two times.
Rnd 30: (P2, K2) two times, P2, K4, (P2, K2) four times, P2, K4, (P2, K2) two times, P2.
Rnd 31: P2, (K2, P2, 2/1 LPC, P1, K4, P1, 2/1 RPC, P2, K2, P2) two times.
Rnd 32: P2, (K2, P3, K2, P1, K4, P1, K2, P3, K2, P2) two times.
Rnd 33: P2, (K2, P3, 2/1 LPC, 2/2 LC, 2/1 RPC, P3, K2, P2) two times.
Rnd 34: P2, (K2, P4, K8, P4, K2, P2) two times.
Rnd 35: P2, *K2, P4, (2/2 RC) two times, P4, K2, P2; rep from * once more.
Rnd 36: P2, (K2, P4, K8, P4, K2, P2) two times.
Rep Rnds 1–36 for pattern.

Chart 2 (in the round over 20 sts)
Rnd 1: P5, 2/1 RPC, 2/2 LC, 2/1 LPC, P5.
Rnd 2: P5, K2, P1, K4, P1, K2, P5.
Rnd 3: P4, 2/1 RPC, P1, K4, P1, 2/1 LPC, P4.
Rnd 4: P4, K2, P2, K4, P2, K2, P4.
Rnd 5: P3, 2/1 RPC, P2, K4, P2, 2/1 LPC, P3.
Rnd 6: P3, K2, P3, K4, P3, K2, P3.
Rnd 7: P2, 2/1 RPC, P3, 2/2 LC, P3, 2/1 LPC, P2.
Rnd 8: P2, K2, P4, K4, P4, K2, P2.
Rnd 9: P2, K2, P3, 2/1 RPC, 2/1 LPC, P3, K2, P2.
Rnd 10: P2, K2, P3, K2, P2, K2, P3, K2, P2.
Rnd 11: P2, K2, P2, 2/1 RPC, P2, 2/1 LPC, P2, K2, P2.
Rnd 12: (P2, K2) two times, P4, (K2, P2) two times.
Rnd 13: P2, K2, P1, 2/1 RPC, P4, 2/1 LPC, P1, K2, P2.
Rnd 14: P2, K2, P1, K2, P6, K2, P1, K2, P2.
Rnd 15: P2, K2, 2/1 RPC, P6, 2/1 LPC, K2, P2.
Rnd 16: P2, K4, P8, K4, P2.
Rnd 17: P2, 2/2 RC, P8, 2/2 RC, P2.
Rnd 18: P2, K4, P8, K4, P2.
Rnd 19: P2, K2, 2/1 LPC, P6, 2/1 RPC, K2, P2.
Rnd 20: P2, K2, P1, K2, P6, K2, P1, K2, P2.
Rnd 21: P2, K2, P1, 2/1 LPC, P4, 2/1 RPC, P1, K2, P2.
Rnd 22: (P2, K2) two times, P4, (K2, P2) two times.
Rnd 23: P2, K2, P2, 2/1 LPC, P2, 2/1 RPC, P2, K2, P2.
Rnd 24: P2, K2, P3, K2, P2, K2, P3, K2, P2.
Rnd 25: P2, K2, P3, 2/1 LPC, 2/1 RPC, P3, K2, P2.
Rnd 26: P2, K2, P4, K4, P4, K2, P2.
Rnd 27: P2, 2/1 LPC, P3, 2/2 LC, P3, 2/1 RPC, P2.
Rnd 28: P3, K2, P3, K4, P3, K2, P3.
Rnd 29: P3, 2/1 LPC, P2, K4, P2, 2/1 RPC, P3.

Rnd 30: P4, K2, P2, K4, P2, K2, P4.
Rnd 31: P4, 2/1 LPC, P1, K4, P1, 2/1 RPC, P4.
Rnd 32: P5, K2, P1, K4, P1, K2, P5.
Rnd 33: P5, 2/1 LPC, 2/2 LC, 2/1 RPC, P5.
Rnd 34: P6, K8, P6.
Rnd 35: P6, (2/2 RC) two times, P6.
Rnd 36: P6, K8, P6.
Rep Rnds 1-36 for pattern.

Chart 2 (flat over 20 sts)
Row 1 (RS): P5, 2/1 RPC, 2/2 LC, 2/1 LPC, P5.
Row 2 (WS): K5, P4, K1, P4, K1, P2, K5.
Row 3: P4, 2/1 RPC, P1, K4, P1, 2/1 LPC, P4.
Row 4: K4, P2, K2, P4, K2, P2, K4.
Row 5: P3, 2/1 RPC, P2, K4, P2, 2/1 LPC, P3.
Row 6: K3, P2, K3, P4, K3, P2, K3.
Row 7: P2, 2/1 RPC, P3, 2/2 LC, P3, 2/1 LPC, P2.
Row 8: K2, P2, K4, P4, K4, P2, K2.
Row 9: P2, K2, P3, 2/1 RPC, 2/1 LPC, P3, K2, P2.
Row 10: K2, P2, K3, P2, K2, P2, K3, P2, K2.
Row 11: P2, K2, P2, 2/1 RPC, P2, 2/1 LPC, P2, K2, P2.
Row 12: (K2, P2) two times, K4, (P2, K2) two times.
Row 13: P2, K2, P1, 2/1 RPC, P4, 2/1 LPC, P1, K2, P2.
Row 14: K2, P2, K1, P2, K6, P2, K1, P2, K2.
Row 15: P2, K2, 2/1 RPC, P6, 2/1 LPC, K2, P2.
Row 16: K2, P4, K8, P4, K2.
Row 17: P2, 2/2 RC, P8, 2/2 RC, P2.
Row 18: K2, P4, K8, P4, K2.
Row 19: P2, K2, 2/1 LPC, P6, 2/1 RPC, K2, P2.
Row 20: K2, P2, K1, P2, K6, P2, K1, P2, K2.
Row 21: P2, K2, P1, 2/1 LPC, P4, 2/1 RPC, P1, K2, P2.
Row 22: (K2, P2) two times, K4, (P2, K2) two times.
Row 23: P2, K2, P2, 2/1 LPC, P2, 2/1 RPC, P2, K2, P2.
Row 24: K2, P2 K3, P2, K2, P2, K3, P2, K2.
Row 25: P2, K2, P3, 2/1 LPC, 2/1 RPC, P3, K2, P2.
Row 26: K2, P2, K4, P4, K4, P2, K2.
Row 27: P2, 2/1 LPC, P3, 2/2 LC, P3, 2/1 RPC, P2.
Row 28: K3, P2, K3, P4, K3, P2, K3.
Row 29: P3, 2/1 LPC, P2, K4, P2, 2/1 RPC, P3.
Row 30: K4, P2, K2, P4, K2, P2, K4.
Row 31: P4, 2/1 LPC, P1, K4, P1, 2/1 RPC, P4.
Row 32: K5, P2, K1, P4, K1, P2, K5.
Row 33: P5, 2/1 LPC, 2/2 LC, 2/1 RPC, P5.
Row 34: K6, P8, K6.
Row 35: P6, (2/2 RC) two times, P6.
Row 36: K6, P8, K6.
Rep Rows 1-36 for pattern.

DIRECTIONS

Body
The body is worked in the round from the bottom up to the underarms.

With smaller size, longer needles, CO 160 (180, 200, 220)(240, 260, 280)(300, 320) sts. PM and join to work in the rnd, being careful not to twist sts.
Work 2x2 Rib for 3".

Switch to larger size needles.
Inc Rnd: *K8 (9, 10, 11)(12, 13, 14)(15, 16), M1; rep from * to end. 180 (200, 220, 240)(260, 280, 300)(320, 340) sts.

Cable Panel Setup Rnd: K22 (27, 32, 37)(42, 47, 52)(57, 62), PM, P2, (K2, P4, K8, P4, K2, P2) two times, PM, K44 (54, 64, 74)(84, 94, 104)(114, 124), PM, P2, (K2, P4, K8, P4, K2, P2) two times, PM, K22 (27, 32, 37)(42, 47, 52)(57, 62).
Cable Panel Rnd 1: K to first M, SM, work Rnd 1 of Chart 1 from chart or written instructions, SM, K to next M, SM, work Rnd 1 of Chart 1, SM, K to end.
Cont as established, working St st outside of Ms and Chart 1 rnds between Ms, until sweater body measures approx 16 (16.5, 16.5, 17)(17.5, 18, 18)(18.5, 18.5)" from CO edge, ending on an even numbered rnd of Chart 1. Do not work last 5 (5, 7, 7)(0, 0, 0)(0, 0) sts of rnd. Do not break yarn. Make note of last rnd worked of Chart 1.

Sleeves (make two the same)
Sleeves are worked in the rnd from cuff up and attached to body at yoke. Begin first sleeve with a new ball of yarn. Read through all directions before beginning sleeve.

Using smaller size DPNs, CO 40 (44, 44, 48)(48, 48, 52)(52, 56) sts. PM and join to work in the rnd, being careful not to twist sts.
Work 2x2 Rib for 3".

Switch to larger size needles.
Next Rnd: K1, M1, K to last st, M1, K1. 42 (46, 46, 50)(50, 50, 54)(54, 58) sts.

Cable Panel Setup Rnd: K11 (13, 13, 15)(15, 15, 17)(17, 19), PM, P6, K8, P6, PM, K11 (13, 13, 15)(15, 15, 17)(17, 19).
Cable Panel Rnd 1: K to first M, SM, work Row 1 of Chart 2 from chart or written instructions, SM, K to end.
Cont as established, working St st outside of Ms and Chart 2 Rows 2-5 (6, 5, 5)(3, 3, 3)(3, 3) between Ms.

On Row 6 (7, 6, 6)(4, 4, 4)(4, 4) of Chart 2, work an Inc Rnd as follows.
Inc Rnd: K1, M1, K to M, SM, work Chart rnd as established, SM, K to last st, M1, K1. 2 sts inc.
Cont as established, working an Inc Rnd every 7 (8, 7, 7)(5, 5, 5)(5, 5) rnds 10 (8, 11, 11)(14, 15, 16)(17, 17) more times. 64 (64, 70, 74)(80, 82, 88)(90, 94) sts.

WE in established pattern until sleeve measures approx 17 (17, 17.5, 17.5)(18, 18, 18.5)(18.5, 19)" from CO edge, ending on an even numbered rnd of Chart 2.

Work first 5 (5, 7, 8)(8, 8, 9)(9, 9) sts of next rnd. Break yarn and place 5 (5, 7, 8)(8, 8, 9)(9, 9) sts before and 5 (5, 7, 8)(8, 8, 9)(9, 9) sts after M onto a st holder or scrap yarn, removing M. Place remaining 54 (54, 56, 58)(64, 66, 70)(72, 76) sts onto separate holder.

End both sleeves on the same rnd of Chart 2, and make note of last pattern row worked.

Yoke

Join sleeves to yoke and work in the rnd as one piece. Switch to larger size 16" circular needles when yoke circumference is too small to fit on 32" needles.

With larger size 32" circular needles and attached ball, join sleeves to body as follows: Place 10 (10, 14, 16)(16, 16, 18)(18, 18) sts of body (last 5 (5, 7, 8)(8, 8, 9)(9, 9) sts of previous rnd and first 5 (5, 7, 8)(8, 8, 9)(9, 9) sts of current rnd) onto holder, PM, K17 (17, 18, 19)(22, 23, 25)(26, 28) sts of first sleeve, SM, work next rnd of Chart 2 as established, SM, K17 (17, 18, 19)(22, 23, 25)(26, 28) sts of first sleeve, PM, K17 (22, 25, 29)(34, 39, 43)(48, 53) sts of body, SM, work next rnd of Chart 1, SM, K17 (22, 25, 29)(34, 39, 43)(48, 53) sts of body, place next 10 (10, 14, 16)(16, 16, 18)(18, 18) sts of body onto holder, PM, K17 (17, 18, 19)(22, 23, 25)(26, 28) sts of second sleeve, SM, work next rnd of Chart 2, SM, K17 (17, 18, 19)(22, 23, 25)(26, 28) sts of second sleeve, PM, K17 (22, 25, 29)(34, 39, 43)(48, 53) sts of body, SM, work next row of Chart 1, SM, K17 (22, 25, 29)(34, 39, 43)(48, 53) sts of body. 268 (288, 304, 324)(356, 380, 404)(428, 456) sts.

Work 2" in established pattern, slipping all Ms.

Body Dec Rnd: K to next M, SM, work next rnd of Chart 2, SM, K to next M, SM, SSK, K to next M, SM, work next rnd of Chart 1, SM, K to 2 sts before M, K2tog, SM, K to next M, SM, work next rnd of Chart 2, SM, K to next M, SM, SSK, K to next M, SM, work next rnd of Chart 1, SM, K to 2 sts before end M, K2tog. 4 sts dec.
Rep Body Dec Rnd 5 (7, 9, 10)(14, 16, 17)(19, 20) more times. 244 (256, 264, 280)(296, 312, 332)(348, 372) sts.

Move placement of the 4 Ms between body and sleeves, each 1 st over into the body section, so that there are now 2 more sts in each sleeve segment and 2 fewer sts on each side of the body, 4 fewer body sts total. Work all decs based on these newly moved Ms.
Sleeve Dec Rnd: SSK, K to next M, SM, work next rnd of Chart 2, SM, K to 2 sts before M, K2tog, SM, K to next M, SM, work next rnd of Chart 1, SM, K to next M, SM, SSK, K to next M, SM, work next rnd of Chart 2, SM, K to 2 sts before M, K2tog, SM, K to next M, SM, work next rnd of Chart 1, SM, K to end. 4 sts dec.
Rep Sleeve Dec Rnd 16 (16, 17, 18)(21, 22, 24)(25, 27) more times. 176 (188, 192, 204)(208, 220, 232)(244, 260) sts.

Move placement of the 4 Ms between body and sleeves, each 1 st over into the sleeve section, so that there are now 2 fewer sts in each sleeve segment, and 2 more sts on each side of the body, 4 more body sts total. Work all decs based on these newly moved Ms. Remove any duplicate Ms.
Second Body Dec Rnd: SM, work next rnd of Chart 2, SM, SSK, K to next M, SM, work next rnd of Chart 1, SM, K to 2 sts before M, K2tog, SM, work next rnd of Chart 2, SM, SSK, K to next M, SM, work next rnd of Chart 1, SM, K to 2 sts before end M, K2tog. 4 sts dec.
Work Second Body Dec Rnd 7 (7, 7, 8) (9, 8, 9) (8, 9) more times. 144 (156, 160, 168)(168, 184, 192)(208, 220) sts.

Make note of last worked rnd of Chart 2. WE in established pattern for one more rnd if necessary to end on an even-numbered chart rnd.

Left Saddle Shoulder
Begin on next consecutive (RS) row of Chart 2 for saddle shoulder, now working Chart 2 flat.

Row 1 (RS): Work next (odd-numbered) row of Chart 2 from chart or written instructions to M, SM, SSK, turn to work flat. 1 st dec.
Row 2 (WS): Sl1 P-wise, SM, work next (even-numbered) row of Chart 2 to M, SM, P2tog, turn. 1 st dec.
Row 3: Sl1 K-wise, SM, work next row of Chart 2 to M, SM, SSK, turn. 1 st dec.
Rep Rows 2-3 another 1 (4, 5, 7)(7, 11, 13)(17, 20) time(s). On final Row 3 rep, do not work dec and do not turn to work flat; cont as follows: SM, K to next M, SM, work next rnd of Chart 1, SM, K to first M of right sleeve.

Right Saddle Shoulder
Begin on next consecutive (RS) row of Chart 2 for saddle shoulder, now working Chart 2 flat.

Row 1 (RS): SM, work next (odd-numbered) row of Chart 2 to M, SM, SSK, turn to work flat. 1 st dec.
Row 2 (WS): Sl1 P-wise, SM, work next (even-numbered) row of Chart 2 to M, SM, P2tog, turn. 1 st dec.
Row 3: Sl1 K-wise, SM, work next row of Chart 2 to M, SM, SSK, turn. 1 st dec.
Rep Rows 2-3 another 1 (4, 5, 7)(7, 11, 13)(17, 20) time(s). On final Row 3 rep, do not work dec and do not turn to work flat; cont as follows: SM, K to next M, SM, work next rnd of Chart 1, SM, K to BOR M.
136 sts remain for all sizes.

Neckband
Switch to smaller size 16" needles. Remove all Ms except BOR M.

Sizes 30 (34, 38, 42)(-, -, -)(-, -)" Only
Setup Rnd: K2tog 16 (10, 10, 4)(-, -, -)(-, -) times, (K2tog, K1) 24 (32, 32, 40)(-, -, -)(-, -) times, K2tog 16 (10, 10, 4)(-, -, -)(-, -) times. 80 (84, 84, 88)(-, -, -)(-, -) sts.

Sizes - (-, -, -)(46, 50, 54)(58, 62)" Only
Setup Rnd: (K2tog, K2) - (-, -, -)(2, 2, 8)(14, 14) times, (K2tog, K1) - (-, -, -)(40, 40, 24)(8, 8) times, (K2tog, K2) - (-, -, -)(2, 2, 8)(14, 14) times. - (-, -, -)(92, 92, 96)(100, 100) sts.

Resume All Sizes
Work 2x2 Rib for 1.5".
BO loosely in pattern.

Finishing
Graft underarm sts tog using Kitchener Stitch.
Weave in ends, wash, and block to diagram.

LEGEND

K
RS: Knit stitch
WS: Purl stitch

P
RS: Purl stitch
WS: Knit stitch

2 over 2 Right Cable (2/2 RC)
Sl2 to CN, hold in back; K2, K2 from CN

2 over 2 Left Cable (2/2 LC)
Sl2 to CN, hold in front; K2, K2 from CN

2 over 1 Right Cable, Purl back (2/1 RPC)
Sl1 to CN, hold in back; K2, P1 from CN

2 over 1 Left Cable, Purl back (2/1 LPC)
Sl2 to CN, hold in front; P1, K2 from CN

Chart 1

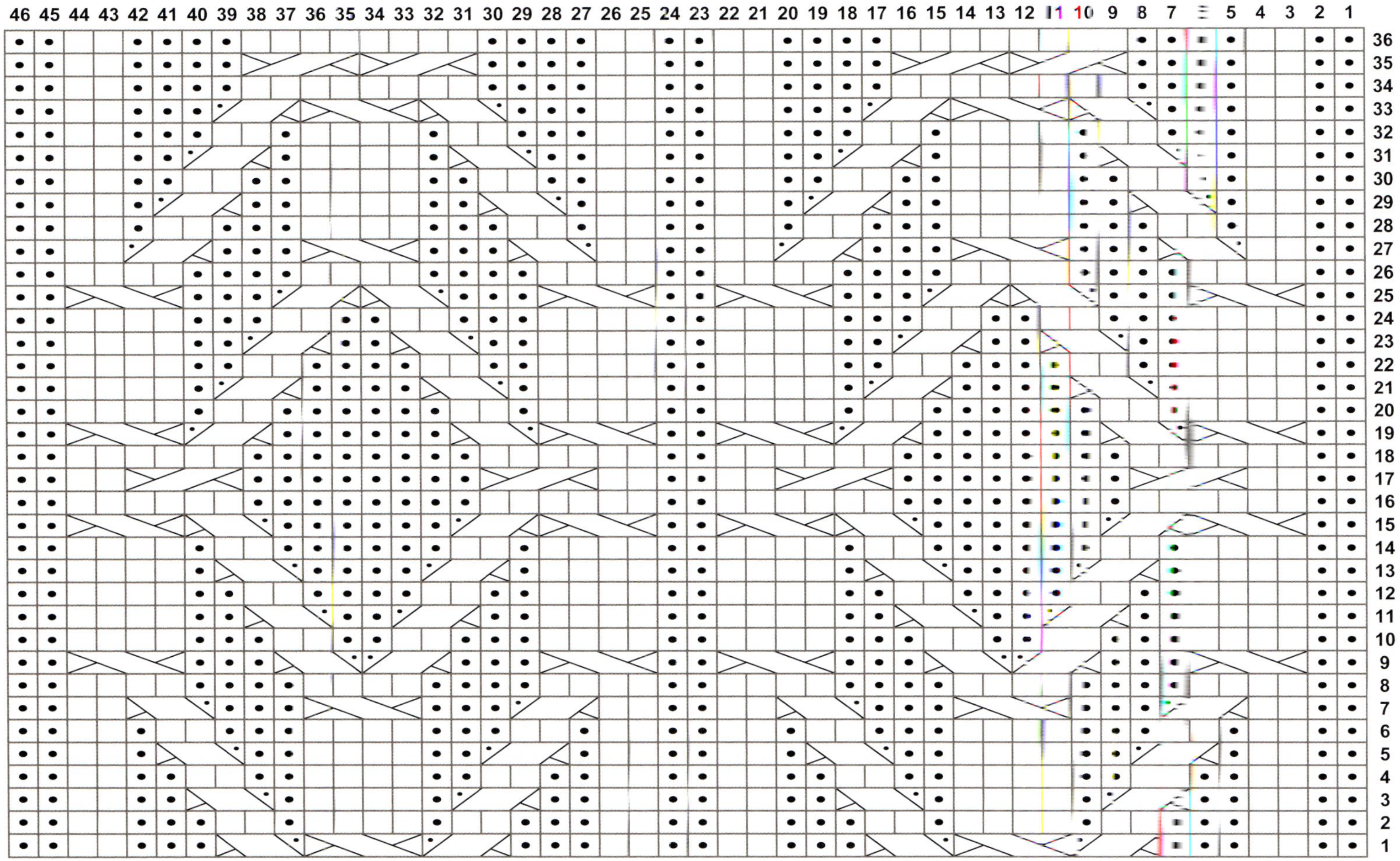

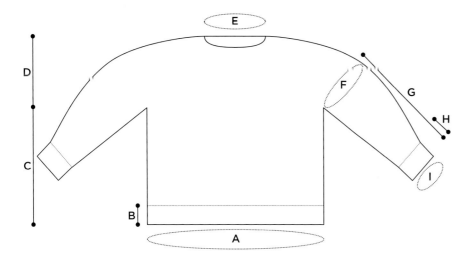

A *body circumference* 30 (34, 38, 42)(46, 50, 54)(58, 62)"
B *rib* 3"
C *length from underarm* 16 (16.5, 16.5, 17)(17.5, 18, 18)(18.5, 18.5)"
D *armhole height* 7.25 (7.5, 8, 8.5)(9.75, 10.25, 10.75)(11.25, 11.75)"
E *neck circumference* 16 (16.75, 16.75, 17.5)(18.5, 18.5, 19.25)(20, 20)"
F *upper arm circumference* 11.5 (11.5, 12.75, 13.5)(14.75, 15, 16.25)(16.75, 17.5)"
G *sleeve length* 17 (17, 17.5, 17.5)(18, 18, 18.5)(18.5, 19)"
H *cuff* 3"
I *wrist circumference* 7.75 (8.25, 8.25, 9.25)(9.25, 9.25, 10)(10, 10.75)"

Chart 2

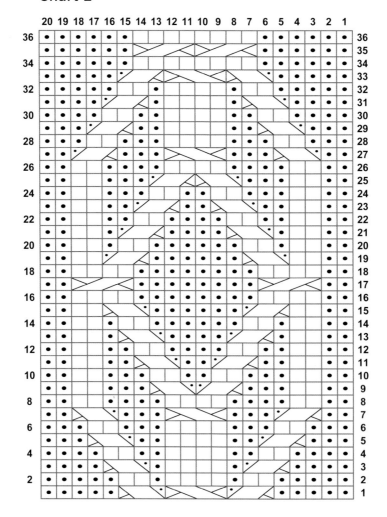

24   Grayrigg Pullover

FLEVILLE WRAP
by Bérangère Cailliau

FINISHED MEASUREMENTS
23.5" width × 63 (68.5, 74)" length
Sample is 68.5" size

YARN
Twill™ (worsted weight, 100% Superwash Merino Wool; 149 yards/100g): Serpent Heather 28535, 9 (10, 11) hanks

NEEDLES
US 7 (4.5mm) straight or circular needles (24" or longer), or one size smaller than size used to obtain gauge
US 8 (5mm) straight or circular needles (24" or longer), or size to obtain gauge

NOTIONS
Yarn Needle
Stitch Markers (2)
Cable Needle
Blocking Pins and/or Wires

GAUGE
16 sts and 25 rows = 4" in Moss Stitch, blocked (gauge is not crucial, but it will affect finished size and yardage requirements)

For pattern support, contact berangere.cailliau@lilofil.com

Fleville Wrap

Notes:

The Fleville wrap was inspired by the geometric patterns from the parquet floors of 16th century castles, such as the castle of Fléville in France.

The Fleville Wrap is a wide rectangular wrap, worked flat from the short end. This unisex wrap consists of Moss Stitch, cables, and a panel of twisted stitches that intersect in the middle.

Charts are worked flat; read RS rows (odd numbers) from right to left, and WS rows (even numbers) from left to right.

2/2 LC (2 over 2 Left Cable)
Sl2 to CN, hold in front; K2, K2 from CN.

2/2 RC (2 over 2 Right Cable)
Sl2 to CN, hold in back; K2, K2 from CN.

LT (Left Twist, without a cable needle)
Sl first st K-wise. Sl second st K-wise; so far, this is as if you are working an SSK decrease. Insert LH needle through both slipped sts, from the bottom up, and Sl them to LH needle like this, so they have become twisted on LH needle. K first (back) st normally. K second (front) st normally.

LPT (Left Twist, Purl back, without a cable needle)
Sl first st K-wise. Sl second stitch K-wise; so far, this is as if you are working an SSK decrease. Insert LH needle through both slipped sts, from the bottom up, and Sl them to LH needle like this, so they have become twisted on LH needle. P first (back) st normally. K second (front) st normally.

RT (Right Twist, without a cable needle)
Insert RH needle through next 2 sts, K-wise tog, as if working K2tog, and Sl them to RH needle like that, so they are now twisted around each other. Sl the 2 sts back over to LH needle, P-wise, so that they stay twisted the same way. K first (front) st TBL (because it is positioned the wrong way on the needle, so this will orient it correctly). K second (back) st TBL.

RPT (Right Twist, Purl back, without a cable needle)
Insert RH needle through next 2 sts, K-wise tog, as if working K2tog and Sl them to RH needle like that, so they are now twisted around each other. Sl the 2 sts back over to LH needle, P-wise, so that they stay twisted the same way. K first (front) st TBL (because it is positioned the wrong way on the needle, so this will orient it correctly). P second (back) st TBL.

Moss Stitch (flat over an even number of sts)
Row 1 (RS): (P1, K1) to end.
Row 2 (WS): Rep Row 1.
Row 3: (K1, P1) to end.
Row 4: Rep Row 3.
Rep Rows 1–4 for pattern.

Fleville Cable Pattern (flat over 67 sts)

Row 1 (RS): Sl1 WYIB, P2, K4, P2, Sl1 WYIB, K1, P2, LPT, (LT) two times, P1, (RT) seven times, RPT, P1, LT, P2, LPT, (LT) two times, P1, (RT) four times, K1, Sl1 WYIB, P2, K4, P2, Sl1 WYIB.
Row 2 (WS): P1, K2, P4, K2, P10, K1, P5, K3, P3, K1, P15, K1, P5, K3, P2, K2, P4, K2, P1.
Row 3: Sl1 WYIB, P2, 2/2 LC, P2, Sl1 WYIB, LT, P2, LPT, LT, P1, (RT) seven times, RPT, P1, (LT) two times, P2, LPT, LT, P1, (RT) five times, Sl1 WYIB, P2, 2/2 RC, P2, Sl1 WYIB.
Row 4: P1, K2, P4, K2, P11, K1, P3, K3, P5, K1, P15, K1, P3, K3, P3, K2, P4, K2, P1.
Row 5: Sl1 WYIB, P2, K4, P2, Sl1 WYIB, K1, LT, P2, LPT, P1, (RT) seven times, RPT, P1, (LT) three times, P2, LPT, P1, (RT) five times, K1, Sl1 WYIB, P2, K4, P2, Sl1 WYIB.
Row 6: P1, K2, P4, K2, P12, K1, P1, K3, P7, K1, P15, K1, P1, K3, (P4, K2) two times, P1.
Row 7: Sl1 WYIB, P2, 2/2 LC, P2, Sl1 WYIB, (LT) two times, P3, (RT) seven times, RPT, P1, (LT) four times, P3, (RT) six times, Sl1 WYIB, P2, 2/2 RC, P2, Sl1 WYIB.
Row 8: P1, K2, P4, K2, P13, K3, P9, K1, P15, K3, P5, K2, P4, K2, P1.
Row 9: Sl1 WYIB, P2, K4, P2, Sl1 WYIB, K1, (LT) two times, P1, (RT) seven times, RPT, P1, (LT) five times, P1, (RT) six times, K1, Sl1 WYIB, P2, K4, P2, Sl1 WYIB.
Row 10: P1, K2, P4, K2, P14, K1, P11, K1, P15, K1, P6, K2, P4, K2, P1.
Row 11: Sl1 WYIB, P2, 2/2 LC, P2, Sl1 WYIB, (LT) three times, P1, (RT) six times, RPT, P1, (LT) six times, P1, (RT) six times, Sl1 WYIB, P2, 2/2 RC, P2, Sl1 WYIB.
Row 12: P1, K2, P4, K2, (P13, K1) three times, P7, K2, P4, K2, P1.
Row 13: Sl1 WYIB, P2, K4, P2, Sl1 WYIB, K1, (LT) three times, P1, (RT) five times, RPT, P1, (LT) seven times, P1, (RT) five times, K1, Sl1 WYIB, P2, K4, P2, Sl1 WYIB.
Row 14: P1, K2, P4, K2, P12, K1, P15, K1, P11, K1, P8, K2, P4, K2, P1.
Row 15: Sl1 WYIB, P2, 2/2 LC, P2, Sl1 WYIB, (LT) four times, P1, (RT) four times, RPT, P1, LPT, (LT) seven times, P1, (RT) four times, RPT, Sl1 WYIB, P2, 2/2 RC, P2, Sl1 WYIB.
Row 16: P1, K2, P4, K2, P1, K1, P9, K1, P15, K3, P9, K1, P9, K2, P4, K2, P1.
Row 17: Sl1 WYIB, P2, K4, P2, Sl1 WYIB, K1, (LT) four times, P1, (RT) three times, RPT, P3, LPT, (LT) seven times, P1, (RT) three times, RPT, P1, Sl1 WYIB, P2, K4, P2, Sl1 WYIB.
Row 18: P1, K2, P4, K2, P1, K2, P7, K1, P15, K1, P1, K3, P7, K1, P10, K2, P4, K2, P1.
Row 19: Sl1 WYIB, P2, 2/2 LC, P2, Sl1 WYIB, (LT) five times, P1, (RT) two times, RPT, P2, RT, P1, LPT, (LT) seven times, P1, (RT) two times, RPT, P2, Sl1 WYIB, P2, 2/2 RC, P2, Sl1 WYIB.
Row 20: P1, K2, P4, K2, P1, K3, P5, K1, P15, K1, P3, K3, P5, K1, P11, K2, P4, K2, P1.
Row 21: Sl1 WYIB, P2, K4, P2, Sl1 WYIB, K1, (LT) five times, P1, RT, RPT, P2, (RT) two times, P1, LPT, (LT) seven times, P1, RT, RPT, P2, K1, Sl1 WYIB, P2, K4, P2, Sl1 WYIB.
Row 22: P1, K2, P4, K2, P2, K3, P3, K1, P15, K1, P5, K3, P3, K1, P12, K2, P4, K2, P1.

Row 23: Sl1 WYIB, P2, 2/2 LC, P2, Sl1 WYIB, (LT) six times, P1, RPT, P2, (RT) three times, P1, LPT, (LT) seven times, P1, RPT, P2, RT, Sl1 WYIB, P2, 2/2 RC, P2, Sl1 WYIB.
Row 24: P1, K2, P4, K2, P3, K3, P1, K1, P15, K1, P7, K3, P1, K1, P13, K2, P4, K2, P1.
Row 25: Sl1 WYIB, P2, K4, P2, Sl1 WYIB, K1, (LT) six times, P3, (RT) four times, P1, LPT, (LT) seven times, P3, RT, K1, Sl1 WYIB, P2, K4, P2, Sl1 WYIB.
Row 26: P1, (K2, P4) two times, K3, P15, K1, P9, K3, P14, K2, P4, K2, P1.
Row 27: Sl1 WYIB, P2, 2/2 LC, P2, Sl1 WYIB, (LT) seven times, P1, (RT) five times, P1, LPT, (LT) seven times, P1, (RT) two times, Sl1 WYIB, P2, 2/2 RC, P2, Sl1 WYIB.
Row 28: P1, K2, P4, K2, P5, K1, P15, K1, P11, K1, P15, K2, P4, K2, P1.
Row 29: Sl1 WYIB, P2, K4, P2, Sl1 WYIB, K1, (LT) six times, P1, (RT) six times, P1, LPT, (LT) six times, P1, (RT) two times, K1, Sl1 WYIB, P2, K4, P2, Sl1 WYIB.
Row 30: P1, K2, P4, K2, P6, (K1, P13) two times, K1, P14, K2, P4, K2, P1.
Row 31: Sl1 WYIB, P2, 2/2 LC, P2, Sl1 WYIB, LPT, (LT) five times, P1, (RT) seven times, P1, LPT, (LT) five times, P1, (RT) three times, Sl1 WYIB, P2, 2/2 RC, P2, Sl1 WYIB.
Row 32: P1, K2, P4, K2, P7, K1, P11, K1, P15, K1, P11, K1, P1, K2, P4, K2, P1.
Row 33: Sl1 WYIB, P2, K4, P2, Sl1 WYIB, P1, LPT, (LT) four times, P1, (RT) seven times, RPT, P1, LPT, (LT) four times, P1, (RT) three times, K1, Sl1 WYIB, P2, K4, P2, Sl1 WYIB.
Row 34: P1, K2, P4, K2, P8, K1, P9, K3, P15, K1, P9, K2, P1, K2, P4, K2, P1.
Row 35: Sl1 WYIB, P2, 2/2 LC, P2, Sl1 WYIB, P2, LPT, (LT) three times, P1, (RT) seven times, RPT, P3, LPT, (LT) three times, P1, (RT) four times, Sl1 WYIB, P2, 2/2 RC, P2, Sl1 WYIB.
Row 36: P1, K2, P4, K2, P9, K1, P7, K3, P1, K1, P15, K1, P7, K3, P1, K2, P4, K2, P1.
Rep Rows 1–36 for pattern.

DIRECTIONS

Beginning Border
With smaller needles, CO 111 sts.
Row 1 (WS): Sl2 WYIF, (P1, K1) to last 3 sts, P1, Sl2 WYIF.
Row 2 (RS): K3, (P1, K1) to last 2 sts, K2.
Rep Rows 1–2 seven more times.

Body
Switch to larger needles.
Setup Row (WS): Sl2 WYIF, (P1, K1) nine times, PM, P1, K2, P3, P2tog, K2, P8, P2tog, P1, K1, P6, K2, P2, K1, P15, P2tog, K1, P6, K2, P2, K2, P3, P2tog, K2, P1, PM, (K1, P1) nine times, Sl2 WYIF. 107 sts.
Row 1 (RS): K2, (P1, K1) to M, SM, work Fleville Cable Pattern Row 1 from chart or written instructions to M, SM, (K1, P1) to last 2 sts, K2.
Row 2: Sl2 WYIF, (K1, P1) to M, SM, work Fleville Cable Pattern Row 2 to M, SM, (P1, K1) to last 2 sts, Sl2 WYIF.
Row 3: K2, (K1, P1) to M, SM, work next row of Fleville Cable Pattern to M, SM, (P1, K1) to last 2 sts, K2.
Row 4: Sl2 WYIF, (P1, K1) to M, SM, work next row of Fleville Cable Pattern to M, SM, (K1, P1) to last 2 sts, Sl2 WYIF.
Cont as established until all rows of Fleville Cable Pattern have been worked 11 (12, 13) times.

Ending Border
Switch to smaller needles.
Row 1 (RS): K3, (P1, K1) to 1 st before M, P1, remove M, (K1, P1) three times, M1R, (P1, K1) five times, P1, M1R, (P1, K1) 14 times, P1, M1R, (P1, K1) eight times, P1, M1R, (P1, K1) to M, remove M, (P1, K1) to last 2 sts, K2. 111 sts.
Row 2 (WS): Sl2 WYIF, (P1, K1) to last 3 sts, P1, Sl2 WYIF.
Row 3: K3, (P1, K1) to last 2 sts, K2.
Rep Rows 2–3 six more times.
Rep Row 2 once more.

BO in pattern.

Finishing
Weave in ends, wash, and block to measurements.

LEGEND

K
- RS: Knit stitch
- WS: Purl stitch

P
- RS: Purl stitch
- WS: Knit stitch

Sl
- Slip stitch purl-wise, with yarn in back

Right Twist (RT)
Sl1 to CN, hold in back; K1, K1 from CN
(or see *Notes* to work without a CN)

Left Twist (LT)
Sl1 to CN, hold in front; K1, K1 from CN
(or see *Notes* to work without a CN)

Right Twist, Purl back (RPT)
Sl1 to CN, hold in back; K1, P1 from CN
(or see *Notes* to work without a CN)

Left Twist, Purl back (LPT)
Sl1 to CN, hold in front; P1, K1 from CN
(or see *Notes* to work without a CN)

2 over 2 Right Cable (2/2 RC)
Sl2 to CN, hold in back; K2, K2 from CN

2 over 2 Left Cable (2/2 LC)
Sl2 to CN, hold in front; K2, K2 from CN

Fleville Cable Pattern

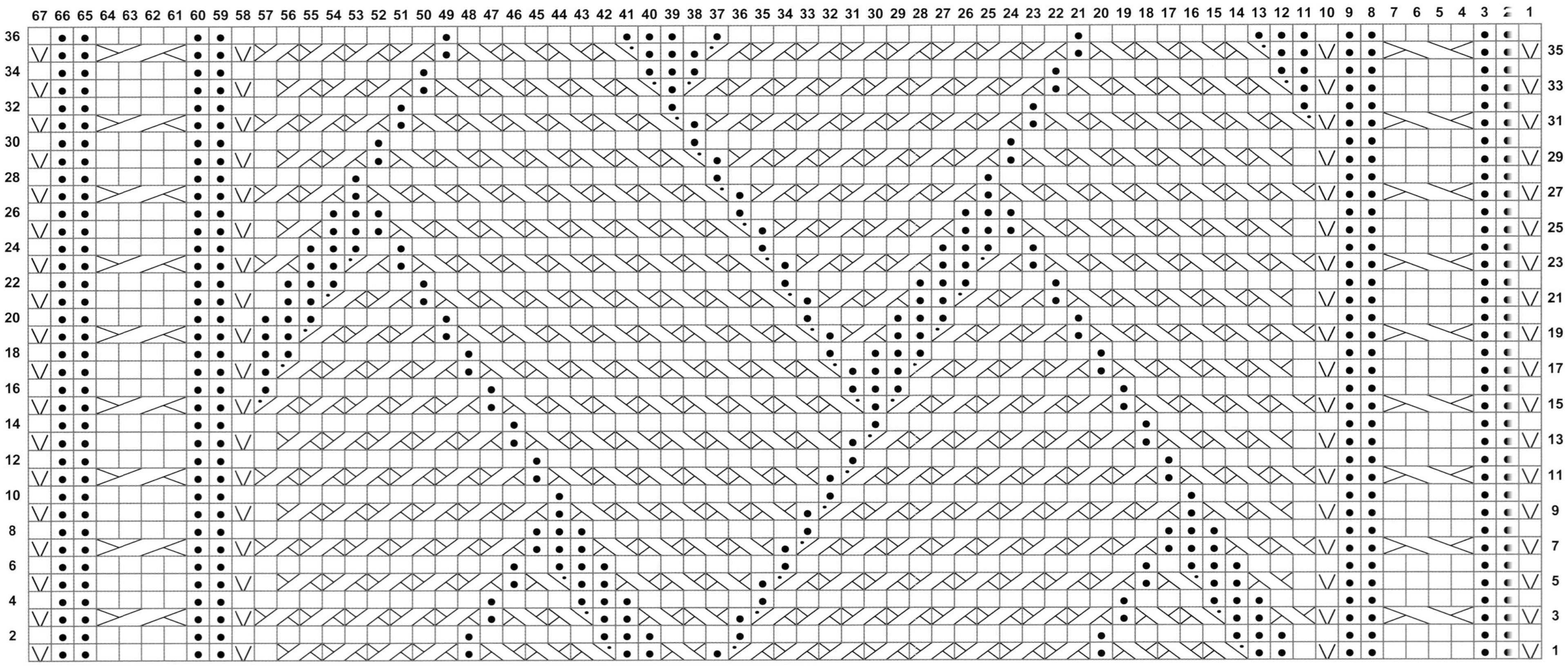

WINTER IVY PULLOVER
by Mari Tobita

FINISHED MEASUREMENTS
33 (37, 42, 46, 51)(56, 60, 64.5, 69)" finished chest circumference; meant to be worn with 3–9" positive ease
Sample is 37"; models are 35"

YARN
Swish™ (DK weight, 100% Fine Superwash Merino Wool; 123 yards/50g): Pinecone Heather 28634, 13 (14, 15, 16, 18)(18, 20, 20, 22) skeins

NEEDLES
US 6 (4mm) straight or circular needles (24" or longer), or size to obtain gauge
US 5 (3.75mm) straight or circular needles (24" or longer), and DPNs or 16" circular needles, or one size smaller than size used to obtain gauge
US 4 (3.5mm) DPN or straight or circular needles for 3-Needle Bind Off

NOTIONS
Yarn Needle
Stitch Markers
Stitch Holders or Scrap Yarn
Cable Needle

GAUGE
19 sts and 29 rows = 4" in Reverse Stockinette Stitch on larger needles, blocked
28 sts and 29 rows = 4" in Cable Pattern A and B on larger needles, blocked

For pattern support, contact maritobita@gmail.com

Winter Ivy Pullover

Notes:
This stitch pattern was inspired by ivy vines and roots seen on a cold winter walk clinging to a brick wall in the gentle sunlight.

All-over cables fill the sweater, which features indented sleeves and is worked back and forth in separate pieces and seamed.

Charts are worked flat; read RS rows (odd numbers) from right to left, and WS rows (even numbers) from left to right.

2/1 LC (2 over 1 Left Cable)
Sl2 to CN, hold in front; K1, K2 from CN.

2/1 RC (2 over 1 Right Cable)
Sl1 to CN, hold in back; K2, K1 from CN.

2/1 LPC (2 over 1 Left Cable, Purl back)
Sl2 to CN, hold in front; P1, K2 from CN.

2/1 RPC (2 over 1 Right Cable, Purl back)
Sl1 to CN, hold in back; K2, P1 from CN.

2/2 LC (2 over 2 Left Cable)
Sl2 to CN, hold in front; K2, K2 from CN.

2/2 RC (2 over 2 Right Cable)
Sl2 to CN, hold in back; K2, K2 from CN.

M1P (Make 1 Purl Stitch)
Inserting LH needle from back to front, PU the horizontal strand between the st just worked and the next st, and P.

Sloped Bind Off
1. One row before next BO row, work to last st of row. Do not work this st. Turn work.
2. Sl first st from LH needle P-wise.
3. Pass unworked st of previous row over Sl st. The first st is bound off.
Cont to BO as usual to desired number of sts for that row.

Cable A—Back and Sleeve (flat over a multiple of 26 sts)
Row 1 (RS): P1, K3, P1, K1, P1, 2/1 LC, P9, 2/1 LPC, 2/1 RPC, P1.
Row 2 and all WS rows: K the K sts and P the P sts.
Row 3: P1, K2, (P1, K1) two times, P1, 2/1 LC, P9, 2/2 RC, P2.
Row 5: P1, K3, (P1, K1) two times, P1, 2/1 LC, P7, 2/1 RPC, 2/1 LC, P1.
Row 7: P1, K2, (P1, K1) three times, P1, 2/1 LC, P5, 2/1 RPC, K1, P1, 2/1 LC.
Row 9: P1, 2/1 LPC, (P1, K1) three times, P1, K2, P4, 2/1 RPC, (K1, P1) two times, K2.
Row 11: P2, 2/1 LPC, (P1, K1) two times, P1, K3, P3, 2/1 RPC, (K1, P1) two times, K3.
Row 13: P3, 2/1 LPC, (P1, K1) two times, P1, K2, P2, 2/1 RPC, (K1, P1) three times, K2.
Row 15: P4, 2/1 LPC, P1, K1, P1, K3, P1, 2/1 RPC, (K1, P1) three times, K3.
Row 17: P5, 2/1 LPC, P1, K1, P1, 2/1 RPC, P1, K3, (P1, K1) three times, 2/1 RPC.
Row 19: P6, 2/1 LPC, 2/1 RPC, P2, K2, (P1, K1) three times, 2/1 RPC, P1.
Row 21: P7, 2/2 RC, P3, K3, (P1, K1) two times, 2/1 RPC, P2.
Row 23: P6, 2/1 RPC, 2/1 LC, P2, K2, (P1, K1) two times, 2/1 RPC, P3.
Row 25: P5, 2/1 RPC, K1, P1, 2/1 LC, P1, K3, P1, K1, 2/1 RPC, P4.
Row 27: P4, 2/1 RPC, (K1, P1) two times, (K2, P1) two times, K1, 2/1 RPC, P5.
Row 29: P3, 2/1 RPC, (K1, P1) two times, K3, P1, 2/1 LPC, 2/1 RPC, P6.
Row 31: P2, 2/1 RPC, (K1, P1) three times, K2, P2, 2/2 RC, P7.
Row 33: P1, 2/1 RPC, (K1, P1) three times, K3, P1, 2/1 RPC, 2/1 LC, P6.
Row 35: P1, K3, (P1, K1) three times, 2/1 RPC, P1, K3, P1, 2/1 LC, P5.
Row 37: P1, K2, (P1, K1) three times, 2/1 RPC, P2, K2, P1, K1, P1, 2/1 LC, P4.
Row 39: P1, K3, (P1, K1) two times, 2/1 RPC, P3, K3, P1, K1, P1, 2/1 LC, P3.
Row 41: P1, K2, (P1, K1) two times, 2/1 RPC, P4, K2, (P1, K1) two times, P1, 2/1 LC, P2.
Row 43: P1, K3, P1, K1, 2/1 RPC, P5, K3, (P1, K1) two times, P1, 2/1 LC, P1
Row 45: P1, K2, P1, K1, 2/1 RPC, P6, K2, (P1, K1) three times, P1, 2/1 LC.
Row 47: P1, 2/1 LPC, 2/1 RPC, P7, 2/1 LPC, (P1, K1) three times, P1, K2.
Row 49: P2, 2/2 RC, P9, 2/1 LPC, (P1, K1) two times, P1, K3.
Row 51: P1, 2/1 RPC, 2/1 LC, P9, 2/1 LPC, (P1, K1) two times, P1, K2.
Row 53: P1, K3, P1, 2/1 LC, P9, 2/1 LPC, P1, K1, P1, K3.
Row 55: P1, K2, P1, K1, P1, 2/1 LC, P9, 2/1 LPC, P1, K1, 2/1 RPC.
Row 56: K1, P3, K1, P2, K10, P3, K1, P1, K1, P2, K1.
Rep Rows 1–56 for pattern.

Cable B—Front (flat over a multiple of 26 sts)
Row 1 (RS): P1, 2/1 LPC, 2/1 RPC, P9, 2/1 RC, P1, K1, P1, K3, P1.
Row 2 and all WS rows: K the K sts and P the P sts.
Row 3: P2, 2/2 LC, P9, 2/1 RC, (P1, K1) two times, P1, K2, P1.
Row 5: P1, 2/1 RC, 2/1 LPC, P7, 2/1 RC, (P1, K1) two times, P1, K3, P1.
Row 7: 2/1 RC, P1, K1, P1, 2/1 LPC, P5, 2/1 RC, (P1, K1) three times, P1, K2, P1.
Row 9: K2, (P1, K1) two times, 2/1 LPC, P4, K2, (P1, K1) three times, P1, 2/1 RPC, P1.
Row 11: K3, (P1, K1) two times, 2/1 LPC, P3, K3, (P1, K1) two times, P1, 2/1 RPC, P2.
Row 13: K2, (P1, K1) three times, 2/1 LPC, P2, K2, (P1, K1) two times, P1, 2/1 RPC, P3.
Row 15: K3, (P1, K1) three times, 2/1 LPC, P1, K3, P1, K1, P1, 2/1 RPC, P4.
Row 17: 2/1 LPC, (K1, P1) three times, K3, P1, 2/1 LPC, K1, P1, 2/1 RPC, P5.
Row 19: P1, 2/1 LPC, (K1, P1) three times, K2, P2, 2/1 LPC, 2/1 RPC, P6.
Row 21: P2, 2/1 LPC, (K1, P1) two times, K3, P3, 2/2 LC, P7.

Row 23: P3, 2/1 LPC, (K1, P1) two times, K2, P2, 2/1 RC, 2/1 LPC, P6.
Row 25: P4, 2/1 LPC, K1, P1, K3, P1, 2/1 RC, P1, K1, 2/1 LPC, P5.
Row 27: P5, 2/1 LPC, K1, (P1, K2) two times, (P1, K1) two times, 2/1 LPC, P4.
Row 29: P6, 2/1 LPC, 2/1 RPC, P1, K3, (P1, K1) two times, 2/1 LPC, P3.
Row 31: P7, 2/1 LPC, P2, K2, (P1, K1) three times, 2/1 LPC, P2.
Row 33: P6, 2/1 RC, 2/1 LPC, P1, K3, (P1, K1) three times, 2/1 LPC, P1.
Row 35: P5, 2/1 RC, P1, K3, P1, 2/1 LPC, (K1, P1) three times, K3, P1.
Row 37: P4, 2/1 RC, P1, K1, P1, K2, P2, 2/1 LPC, (K1, P1) three times, K2, P1.
Row 39: P3, 2/1 RC, P1, K1, P1, K3, P3, 2/1 LPC, (K1, P1) two times, K3, P1.
Row 41: P2, 2/1 RC, (P1, K1) two times, P1, K2, P4, 2/1 LPC, (K1, P1) two times, K2, P1.
Row 43: P1, 2/1 RC, (P1, K1) two times, P1, K3, P5, 2/1 LPC, K1, P1, K3, P1.
Row 45: 2/1 RC, (P1, K1) three times, P1, K2, P6, 2/1 LPC, K1, P1, K2, P1.
Row 47: K2, (P1, K1) three times, P1, 2/1 RPC, P7, 2/1 LPC, 2/1 RPC, P1.
Row 49: K3, (P1, K1) two times, P1, 2/1 RPC, P9, 2/2 LC, P2.
Row 51: K2, (P1, K1) two times, P1, 2/1 RPC, P9, 2/1 RC, 2/1 LPC, P1.
Row 53: K3, P1, K1, P1, 2/1 RPC, P9, 2/1 RC, P1, K3, P1.
Row 55: 2/1 LPC, K1, P1, 2/1 RPC, P9, 2/1 RC, P1, K1, P1, K2, P1.
Row 56: K1, P2, K1, P1, K1, P3, K10, P2, K1, P3, K1.
Rep Rows 1–56 for pattern.

DIRECTIONS

The selvage sts are included in the written instructions; Sl Ms as you come to them.

Back
With smaller needles and Long Tail Cast On method, CO 122 (130, 154, 162, 182)(206, 218, 238, 246) sts.

Hem
Sizes 33 (37, -, -, -)(56, -, -, -)" Only
Setup Row (WS): (K2, P2) to last 2 sts, K2.
Row 1 (RS): K1, P1, (K2, P2) to last 4 sts, K2, P1, K1.
Row 2: (K2, P2) to last 2 sts, K2.
Rows 3–15: Rep Rows 1–2 six more times, then Row 1 once more.
Row 16 (WS): K1, (K1, P2, K1) 1 (2, -, -, -)(1, -, -, -) time(s), *PM, K1, (P2, K2) four times, (P2, K2tog) two times, P2, K1; rep from * 3 (3, -, -, -)(6, -, -, -) more times, PM, (K1, P2, K1) 1 (2, -, -, -)(1, -, -, -) time(s), K1. 114 (122, -, -, -)(192, -, -, -) sts.

Sizes - (-, 42, 46, 51)(-, 60, 64.5, 69)" Only
Setup Row (WS): K1, P1, (K2, P2) to last 4 sts, K2, P1, K1.
Row 1 (RS): (K2, P2) to last 2 sts, K2.
Row 2: K1, P1, (K2, P2) to last 4 sts, K2, P1, K1.
Rows 3–15: Rep Rows 1–2 six more times, then Row 1 once more.
Row 16 (WS): K1, P1, K1, (K1, P2, K1) - (-, 1, 2, 1)(-, 2, 1, 2) time(s), *PM, K1, (P2, K2) four times, (P2, K2tog) two times, P2, K1; rep from * - (-, 4, 4, 5)(-, 6, 7, 7) more times, PM, (K1, P2, K1) - (-, 1, 2, 1)(-, 2, 1, 2) time(s), K1, P1, K1. - (-, 144, 152, 170)(-, 204, 222, 230) sts.

Body
Change to larger needles. Begin Cable A pattern.

Sizes 33 (37, 42, 46, -)(-, 60, 64.5, -)" Only
Row 1 (RS): K1, P4 (8, 6, 10, -)(-, 10, 6, -), work Row 1 of Cable A from chart or written instructions 4 (4, 5, 5, -)(-, 7, 8, -) times, P4 (8, 6, 10, -)(-, 10, 6, -), M1P, K1. 115 (123, 145, 153, -)(-, 205, 223, -) sts.

Sizes - (-, -, -, 51)(56, -, -, 69)" Only
Row 1 (RS): K1, P- (-, -, -, 6)(4, -, -, 10), M1P, work Row 1 of Cable A from chart or written instructions - (-, -, -, 6)(7, -, -, 8) times, M1P, P- (-, -, -, 6)(4, -, -, 10), M1P, K1. - (-, -, -, 173)(195, -, -, 233) sts.

Resume All Sizes
Row 2 (WS): K to M, work Row 2 of Cable A to last M, K to end.
Row 3 (RS): K1, P to M, work next row of Cable A to last M, P to last st, K1.
Row 4: K to M, work next row of Cable A to last M, K to end.
Rep Rows 3–4 as established through Row 56 of Cable A pattern.

Cont as established, rep pattern Rows 1–38 (42, 38, 34, 32)(30, 28, 24, 22) once more.
Piece measures 15 (15.5, 15, 14.5, 14.25)(13.75, 13.5, 13, 12.75)" from CO edge.

Armhole
Working as established, BO 4 (5, 5, 6, 7)(5, 7, 6, 8) sts at beginning of next two rows. 107 (113, 135, 141, 159)(185, 191, 211, 217) sts.
Cont in pattern as established through last row of chart.
Rep Chart Rows 1–34 (42, 42, 42, 42)(44, 46, 46, 48) once more.

Neck & Shoulder
Next Row (RS): Work 32 (35, 45, 46, 53)(66, 67, 77, 79) sts, BO 43 (43, 45, 49, 53)(53, 57, 57, 59) sts, work to end.
Next Row (WS): Work in pattern to center BO.
Place all just-worked sts of left shoulder onto st holder or scrap yarn.
With WS facing, join new yarn to live sts at beginning of center BO. Work in pattern for one row.
Place all just-worked sts of right shoulder onto st holder or scrap yarn.
Piece measures 7.5 (8, 8.5, 9, 9.25)(10, 10.5, 11, 11.5)" from Armhole BO.

Front
With smaller needles, CO 122 (130, 154, 162, 182)(206, 218, 238, 246) sts using Long Tail Cast On.

Hem

Sizes 33 (37, -, -, -)(56, -, -, -)" Only
Work as for Back through Row 15.
Row 16 (WS): K1, (K1, P2, K1) 1 (2, -, -, -)(1, -, -, -) time(s), *PM, K1, (P2, K2tog) two times, (P2, K2) four times, P2, K1; rep from * 3 (3, -, -, -)(6, -, -, -) more times, PM, (K1, P2, K1) 1 (2, -, -, -)(1, -, -, -) time(s), K1. 114 (122, -, -, -)(192, -, -, -) sts.

Sizes - (-, 42, 46, 51)(-, 60, 64.5, 69)" Only
Setup Row (WS): K1, P1, (K2, P2) to last 4 sts, K2, P1, K1.
Row 1 (RS): (K2, P2) to last 2 sts, K2.
Row 2 : K1, P1, (K2, P2) to last 4 sts, K2, P1, K1.
Rep Rows 1–2 six more times, then Row 1 once more.
Row 16 (WS): K1, P1, K1, (K1, P2, K1) - (-, 1, 2, 1)(-, 2, 1, 2) time(s), *PM, K1, (P2, K2tog) two times, (P2, K2) four times, P2, K1; rep from * - (-, 4, 4, 5)(-, 6, 7, 7) more times, PM, (K1, P2, K1) - (-, 1, 2, 1)(-, 2, 1, 2) time(s), K1, P1, K1. - (-, 144, 152, 170)(-, 204, 222, 230) sts.

Body
Change to larger needles. Begin Cable B pattern.

Sizes 33 (37, 42, 46, -)(-, 60, 64.5, -)" Only
Row 1 (RS): K1, M1P, P4 (8, 6, 10, -)(-, 10, 6, -), work Row 1 of Cable B from chart or written instructions 4 (4, 5, 5, -)(-, 7, 8, -) times, P4 (8, 6, 10, -)(-, 10, 6, -), K1. 115 (123, 145, 153, -)(-, 205, 223, -) sts.

Sizes - (-, -, -, 51)(56, -, -, 69)" Only
Row 1 (RS): K1, M1P, P- (-, -, -, 6)(4, -, -, 10), M1P, work Row 1 of Cable B from chart or written instructions - (-, -, -, 6)(7, -, -, 8) times, M1P, P- (-, -, -, 6)(4, -, -, 10), K1. - (-, -, -, 173)(195, -, -, 233) sts.

Resume All Sizes
Row 2 (WS): K to M, work Row 2 of Cable B to last M, K to end.
Row 3 (RS): K1, P to M, work next row of Cable B to last M, P to last st, K1.
Row 4: K to M, work next row of Cable B to last M, K to end.

Cont working same as for Back using Cable B pattern until two 56-row reps of pattern have been completed from CO edge. 107 (113, 135, 141, 159)(185, 191, 211, 217) sts.
Work 2 (10, 10, 10, 10)(12, 14, 14, 16) more rows in pattern, ending with a WS Row.

Left Neck Edge Shaping
Row 1 (RS): Work 47 (50, 60, 62, 71)(84, 84, 94, 97) sts, BO 13 (13, 15, 17, 17)(17, 23, 23, 23) sts, work to end. Leave first set of worked sts on cable for later, working only the left side sts.
Row 2 (WS): Work to last st, turn.
Use Sloped Bind Off method on following rows.
Working as established, at beginning of RS rows: BO 5 (5, 5, 5, 6)(6, 6, 6, 6) sts once, BO 4 (4, 4, 4, 5)(5, 4, 4, 4) sts once, BO 3 sts once, BO 2 sts once, BO 1 st 1 (1, 1, 2, 2)(2, 2, 2, 3) time(s). 32 (35, 45, 46, 53)(66, 67, 77, 79) sts.
WE as established for 23 (23, 23, 21, 21)(21, 21, 21, 19) more rows, ending on a WS Row.
Place 32 (35, 45, 46, 53)(66, 67, 77, 79) shoulder sts onto st holder or scrap yarn.

Right Neck Edge Shaping
With WS facing, join new yarn to live sts at beginning of center BO.
Working as established, at beginning of WS rows: BO 5 (5, 5, 5, 6)(6, 6, 6, 6) sts once, BO 4 (4, 4, 4, 5)(5, 4, 4, 4) sts once, BO 3 sts once, BO 2 sts once, BO 1 st 1 (1, 1, 2, 2)(2, 2, 2, 3) time(s). 32 (35, 45, 46, 53)(66, 67, 77, 79) sts.
WE as established for 24 (24, 24, 22, 22)(22, 22, 22, 20) more rows, ending on a WS Row.
Place 32 (35, 45, 46, 53)(66, 67, 77, 79) shoulder sts onto st holder or scrap yarn.

Sleeves (make two the same)
Before you start, read through this section, as incs happen at the same time as Cable A pattern. Incs are worked inside of 2 side sts. If there are not enough sts to make cables, substitute K or P sts.
All sizes begin with two 26-st reps of Cable A pattern; incs at side edges will make for 3 (3, 3, 4, 4)(4, 4, 4, 4) full reps of cable pattern. Remaining sts on either side are worked in Rev St st.

Cuff
With smaller needles, CO 62 (62, 70, 70, 70)(78, 78, 86, 86) sts using Long Tail Cast On.
Setup Row (WS): K1, P1, (K2, P2) to last 4 sts, K2, P1, K1.
Row 1 (RS): K2, P2, (K2, P2) to last 2 sts, K2.
Row 2 : K1, P1, (K2, P2) to last 4 sts, K2, P1, K1.
Rows 3–13: Rep Rows 1–2 five more times, then Row 1 once more.

Sizes 33 (37, -, -, -)(-, -, -, -)" Only
Row 14 (WS): K1, P1, K1, *PM, K1, (P2, K2) four times (P2, K2tog) two times, P2, K1; rep from * once more, PM, K1, P1, K1. 58 sts.

Sizes - (-, 42, 46, 51)(-, -, -, -)" Only
Row 14 (WS): K1, P1, K2, P2, K1, *PM, K1, (P2, K2) four times (P2, K2tog) two times, K1; rep from * once more, PM, K1, P2, K2, P1, K1. 66 sts.

Sizes - (-, -, -, -)(56, 60, -, -)" Only
Row 14 (WS): K1, P1, (K2, P2) two times, K1, *PM, K1, (P2, K2) four times (P2, K2tog) two times, K1; rep from * once more, PM, K1, (P2, K2) two times, P1, K1. 74 sts.

Sizes - (-, -, -, -)(-, -, 64.5, 69)" Only
Row 14 (WS): K1, P1, K2, (P2, K2tog) two times, P2, K1, *PM, K1, (P2, K2) four times (P2, K2tog) two times, K1; rep from * once more, PM, K1, (P2, K2,) three times, P1, K1. 80 sts.

Sleeve Shaping
Change to larger needles.
Begin Cable A pattern from Sleeve Chart, working appropriate pattern for size.

Sizes 33 (37, -, -, -)(-, -, -, -)" Only
Row 1 (RS): K2, PM, P1, SM, work Row 1 of Cable A two times, SM, P1, M1P, PM, K2. 59 sts.

Sizes - (-, 42, 46, 51)(-, -, -, -)" Only
Row 1 (RS): K2, PM, K1, 2/1 RPC, P1, SM, work Row 1 of Cable A two times, SM, P1, K3, P1, M1P, PM, K2. 67 sts.

Sizes - (-, -, -, -)(56, 60, -, -)" Only
Row 1 (RS): K2, PM, P2, 2/1 LPC, 2/1 RPC, P1, SM, work Row 1 of Cable A two times, SM, P1, K3, (P1, K1) two times, P1, M1P, PM, K2. 75 sts.

Sizes - (-, -, -, -)(-, -, 64.5, 69)" Only
Row 1 (RS): K1, SSK, PM, P5, 2/1 LPC, 2/1 RPC, P1, SM, work Row 1 of Cable A two times, SM, P1, K3, P1, K1, P1, 2/1 LPC, M1P, P1, M1P, PM, K2. 81 sts.

Resume All Sizes
Row 2 (WS): K1, K the K sts and P the P sts to last st, K1.

Cont in pattern as established (working incs as given below) until 2 (2, 2, 2, 2)(2, 2, 1, 1) rep(s) of Cable A pattern have been completed.
Rep Rows 1–30 (28, 20, 16, 14)(4, 2, 50, 48).

AT THE SAME TIME inc at both edges as follows, starting on cable pattern Row 7 (5, 7, 5, 3)(3, 3, 3, 3).
Inc Row (RS): K2, M1P, work to last 2 sts, M1P, K2. 2 sts inc.
Rep Inc Row every RS row - (-, -, -, 3)(4, 9, 13, 19) more times, every four rows - (2, -, 26, 26)(23, 20, 16, 12) times, every six rows 15 (19, 19, -, -)(-, -, -, -) times, then every eight rows 4 (-, -, -, -)(-, -, -, -) times. 99 (103, 107, 121, 127)(131, 135, 141, 145) sts.

WE until piece measures 21.5 (21, 20, 19.5, 19.25)(17.75, 17.5, 16.25, 16)" from CO edge.
BO all sts.

Finishing
Wash and block all pieces to measurements.
Join shoulders of front and back, using 3-Needle Bind Off method with smallest needle.
Place each end of top of sleeves at armhole on front and back and sew sleeves to body.
Sew sides of body and sleeve seams.

Neckband
With smaller DPNs or 16" circular needles, and beginning at right corner of back neck, PU and K 40 (40, 40, 44, 44)(44, 46, 46, 52) sts along back neck, PU and K 80 (84, 84, 84, 88)(88, 90, 90, 92) sts along front neck. 120 (124, 124, 128, 132)(132, 136, 136, 144) sts.
Join to work in the rnd and PM for BOR.
Purl one rnd.

Work 2x2 Rib for eleven rnds.
BO all sts loosely in pattern.
Weave in all ends.

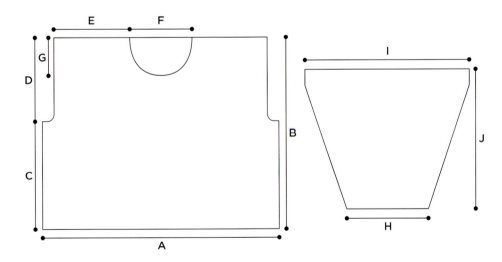

- A *chest width* 17 (19, 21.5, 23.5, 26)(28.5, 30.5, 32.75, 35)"
- B *body length* 22.5 (23.5, 23.5, 23.5, 23.5)(23.75, 24, 24, 24.25)"
- C *side seam* 15 (15.5, 15, 14.5, 14.25)(13.75, 13.5, 13, 12.75)"
- D *armhole depth* 7.5 (8, 8.5, 9, 9.25)(10, 10.5, 11, 11.5)"
- E *shoulder* 4.75 (5.25, 6.5, 7, 7.75)(9.5, 9.75, 11, 11.5)"
- F *neck width* 6 (6.25, 6.5, 7, 7.5)(7.5, 8, 8.25, 8.5)"
- G *neck depth* 4.75"
- H *wrist* 8.5 (8.5, 9.5, 9.5, 9.5)(10.75, 10.75, 11.5, 11.5)"
- I *upper arm width* 15.25 (16.25, 17.25, 18.5, 19.5)(20.5, 21.5, 22.5, 23.5)"
- J *sleeve length* 21.25 (21, 20, 19.5, 19.25)(17.75, 17.5, 16.25, 16)"

Cable A—Back and Sleeve

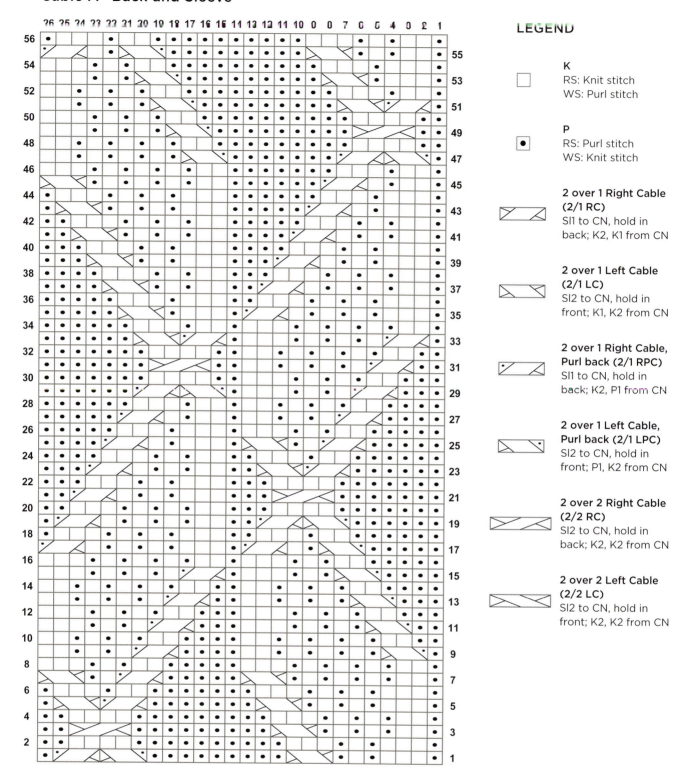

Cable A—Sleeve Layout Reference

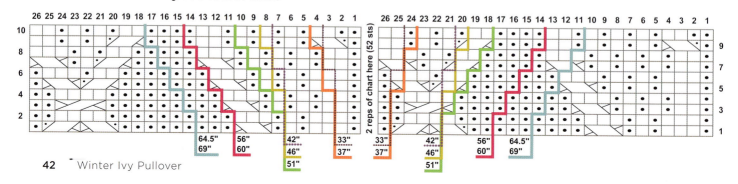

Cable B—Front

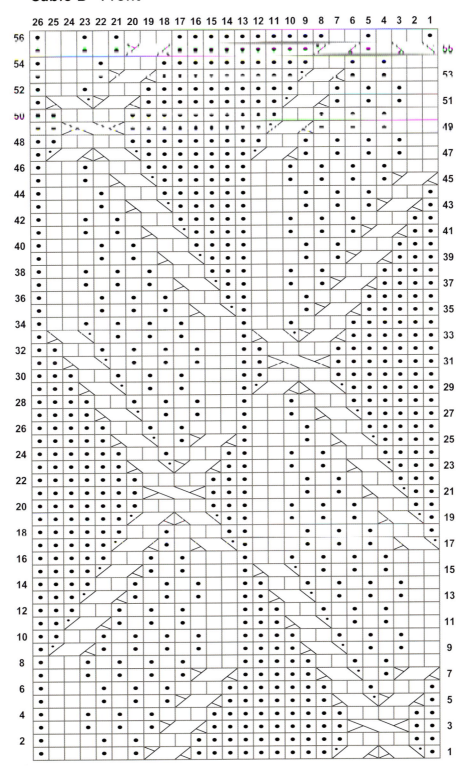

Winter Ivy Pullover

KORZINA COWL
by Lisa Ebert

FINISHED MEASUREMENTS
55" circumference (customizable) × 6" height

YARN
Simply Wool™ (bulky, 100% Eco Wool; 193 yards/100g): Wilbur 27482, 2 hanks

NEEDLES
US 10 (6mm) straight or circular needles

NOTIONS
Yarn Needle
Cable Needle
Spare Circular or Straight Needle (smaller size than working needles)
Scrap Yarn or Stitch Holder

GAUGE
28 sts and 28 rows = 4" in Korzina Pattern, blocked (gauge is not crucial, but it will affect finished size and yardage requirements)

For pattern support, contact lisa.e.ebert@gmail.com

Korzina Cowl

Notes:

There's nothing cozier than a double-looped, cabled cowl on a cool night. This woven-textured cowl allows the wearer to loop a cabled piece with confidence — the "wrong" side is just as fun to look at as the right side!

This cowl is knit flat, then joined together with stitch-by-stitch grafting directions. It's intended to be long enough for a double loop around the neck, but the simple 6-stitch, 8-row repeat means it's easy to make wider, narrower, shorter, or longer. It can even be left un-joined for a scarf, or shortened for a single-loop fit.

Chart is worked flat; read RS rows (odd numbers) from right to left, and WS rows (even numbers) from left to right.

F (used in Joining) = Front

R (used in Joining) = Rear

Turkish Provisional Cast On for 2 Circular Needles
One set of circulars is the working set. The other set is the stitch holder for the provisional sts. The stitch holder set can be smaller than the working set.
Create a slip knot and put it on your stitch holder needle. Hold one needle from the working set and one from the stitch holder set tog and pointed to the right, so the stitch holder needle with the slip knot is below.
Bring the yarn behind the needles, and wrap it around the pair. 1 st CO.
Wrap the needles as many times as needed. The slip knot does not count as a st, it is simply anchoring the sts.
Pull the stitch holder needle to the right (through the sts) so the sts are on the working needle and the cable of the circular needle.
Work first row of the pattern using the sts on the working needle. The sts on the circular cable will remain until it is time to graft them.

Turkish Provisional Cast On for Straight Needles
Hold the two needles tog, points to the right, one above the other.
Create a slip knot and place it on the lower needle.
Bring the yarn behind the needles and wrap it around the pair. 1 st CO.
Wrap the needles as many times as needed. The slip knot does not count as a st, it is simply anchoring the sts.
Pull out the lower needle and replace it with a stitch holder or scrap yarn.
Work the first row of the pattern using the sts on the upper needle. The sts on the stitch holder will rem until it is time to graft them.

3/3 RRC (3 over 3 Right Ribbed Cable)
Sl3 sts to CN, hold in back; (K1, P1, K1) from needle, then (K1, P1, K1) from CN.

3/3 LRC (3 over 3 Left Ribbed Cable)
Sl3 sts to CN, hold in front; (K1, P1, K1) from needle, then (K1, P1, K1) from CN.

Korzina Pattern (flat over 39 sts)
Setup Row (WS): K1, P1, K1, (P1, K1, P1) eleven times, K1, P1, K1.
Row 1 (RS): Sl1 WYIF, P1, K2, P1, K1, (3/3 LRC) five times, K1, P1, K1.
Row 2 and all WS Rows: Sl1 WYIF, P1, K1, (P1, K1, P1) eleven times, K1, P1, K1.
Row 3: Sl1 WYIF, P1, K1, (K1, P1, K1) eleven times, K1, P1, K1.
Row 5: Sl1 WYIF, P1, K1, (3/3 RRC) five times, (K1, P1, K1) two times.
Row 7: Rep Row 3.
Rep Rows 1–8 for pattern.

DIRECTIONS
Using Turkish Provisional Cast On, CO 39 sts.

Following Korzina Pattern chart or written instructions, work Setup Row.
Rep Rows 1–8 until piece measures approx 55", ending on pattern Row 6.

Joining
Measure out a length of yarn approx 21", cut yarn, thread into yarn needle.
Place held CO sts onto second needle, so both needles are pointing right and cowl fabric is RS facing out and not twisted. Needle with CO sts should be held to the rear, needle with last worked sts in front.

Graft ends tog as follows.
St 1F: Insert yarn needle into first front st, K-wise.
St 1R: Insert yarn needle into first rear st, K-wise.
St 1–2F: Insert needle into front st P-wise, remove st from needle. Insert needle into next st K-wise.
Rep St 1–2F for rear needle sts.

St 2–3F: Insert needle into front st P-wise, remove st from needle. Insert needle into next st P-wise.
Rep St 2–3F for rear needle sts.

St 3–4F: Insert needle into front st K-wise, remove st from needle. Insert needle into next st P-wise.
St 3–4R: Insert needle into rear st K-wise, remove st from needle. Insert needle into next st K-wise.
St 4–5F: Insert needle into front st K-wise, remove st from needle. Insert needle into next st K-wise.
St 4–5R: Insert needle into rear st P-wise, remove st from needle. Insert needle into next st P-wise.
St 5–6F: Insert needle into front st P-wise, remove st from needle. Insert needle into next st P-wise.

St 5-6R: Insert needle into rear st K-wise, remove st from needle. Insert needle into next st K-wise.

St 6-7F: Insert needle into front st K-wise, remove st from needle. Insert needle into next st P-wise.

St 6-7R: Insert needle into rear st P-wise, remove st from needle. Insert needle into next st K-wise.

Rep St 4-5F to St 6-7R until 3 sts remain on front needle, 4 remain on rear needle, ending on st 6-7F.

St 36-37R: Insert needle into rear st P-wise, remove st from needle. Insert needle into next st P-wise.

St 37-38F: Insert needle into front st K-wise, remove st from needle. Insert needle into next st K-wise.
Rep St 37-38F for rear needle sts.

St 38-39F: Insert needle into front st P-wise, remove st from needle. Insert needle into next st P-wise.
Rep St 38-39F for rear needle sts.

St 39F: Insert needle into front st K-wise, remove st from needle.
Rep St 39F for rear needle st.

Finishing

To even out the tension of grafted sts, use yarn needle to tug legs of joined sts as needed until all sts are approx the same size.

Weave in ends, wash, and block to dimensions.

LEGEND

K
RS: Knit stitch
WS: Purl stitch

P
RS: Purl stitch
WS: Knit stitch

Sl WYIF
RS: Slip stitch purl-wise, with yarn in front

Sl WYIF on WS
WS: Slip stitch purl-wise, with yarn in front

3 over 3 Right Ribbed Cable (3/3 RRC)
Sl 3 sts to CN, hold in back; (K1, P1, K1) from needle, then (K1, P1, K1) from CN

3 over 3 Left Ribbed Cable (3/3 LRC)
Sl 3 sts to CN, hold in front; (K1, P1, K1) from needle, then (K1, P1, K1) from CN

Korzina Pattern

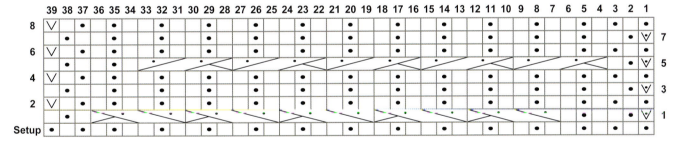

TREELINE SWEATER
by Camilyn Crane

FINISHED MEASUREMENTS
33.5 (36.25, 39, 44.5, 47.25)(52.75, 55.75, 61.25, 64)" finished chest circumference; meant to be worn with 2-4" positive ease *Samples are 36.25" (brown) & 44.5" (red); models are 35" except short-haired male model is 38"*

YARN
Wool of the Andes™ Tweed (worsted weight, 80% Peruvian Highland Wool, 20% Donegal Tweed; 110 yards/50g): Rabbit Heather 25455 or Barn Door Heather 25454, 11 (11, 13, 14, 15)(16, 18, 19, 21) skeins

NEEDLES
US 8 (5mm) 32" circular needles, or size to obtain gauge

US 8 (5mm) DPNs or 16" circular needles (for sizes 52.75", 55.75", 61.25", and 64") for cabled sleeves, or size to obtain gauge
US 7 (4.5mm) DPNs or 16" circular needles (for sizes 52.75", 55.75", 61.25", and 64") for optional Stockinette Stitch sleeves

NOTIONS
Yarn Needle
Removable Stitch Markers (6)
Cable Needle
Scrap Yarn or Stitch Holder
Blocking Pins and/or Wires

GAUGE
23 sts and 22 rows = 4" in Pine Cable Pattern in the round and flat, blocked
18 sts and 22 rnds = 4" in Stockinette Stitch in the round on smaller needles, blocked

For pattern support, contact goldenpinecreations@gmail.com

Treeline Sweater

Notes:

Inspired by the impressive mountains at the border between Idaho and Wyoming, the line of pine trees on the sweater is reminiscent of the forest as seen from the bare, snowy tops of the mountains.

The Treeline Sweater is a seamless set-in sleeve sweater, knit from the bottom up. Instead of knitting the sleeves separately, the top-down set-in sleeve method is used after joining the shoulders. The cable pattern is a simple 16-stitch wide and 6-row repeat, with the option to use that or Stockinette Stitch for the sleeves.

Chart is worked both in the round and flat. When working chart in the round, read each chart row from right to left as a RS row; when working chart flat, read RS rows (odd numbers) from right to left, and WS rows (even numbers) from left to right.

2/2 RC (2 over 2 Right Cable)
Sl2 sts to CN and hold in back; K2, K2 from CN.

2/2 LC (2 over 2 Left Cable)
Sl2 sts to CN and hold in front; K2, K2 from CN.

Pine Cable (in the round over a multiple of 16 sts)
Rnd 1: K4, 2/2 RC, 2/2 LC, K4.
Rnd 2 and all even numbered rnds: K all.
Rnd 3: K2, 2/2 RC, K4, 2/2 LC, K2.
Rnd 5: 2/2 RC, K8, 2/2 LC.
Rep Rnds 1–6 for pattern.

Pine Cable (flat over a multiple of 16 sts)
Row 1 (RS): K4, 2/2 RC, 2/2 LC, K4.
Row 2 and all WS Rows: P all.
Row 3: K2, 2/2 RC, K4, 2/2 LC, K2.
Row 5: 2/2 RC, K8, 2/2 LC.
Rep Rows 1–6 for pattern.

DIRECTIONS

Body

Loosely CO 144 (160, 176, 208, 208)(240, 256, 288, 304) sts using CO method of your choice. PM for BOR and join in the rnd, being careful not to twist sts.

Work 1x1 Rib for 2". On final rnd, work 72 (80, 88, 104, 104)(120, 128, 144, 152) sts, PM for middle, work to end.

Setup Rnd: K all sts while inc 48 (48, 48, 48, 64)(64, 64, 64, 64) sts evenly, using the following instructions for size being made. Sl middle M's as you come to them.
Size 33.5": K1, (M1L, K3) 47 times, M1L, K2. 192 sts.
Sizes 36.25" & 39": K2, (M1L, K3) 16 (8) times, (M1L, K4) 15 (31) times, (M1L, K3) 16 (8) times, M1L, K2. 208 (224) sts.
Size 44.5": K2, (M1L, K5) eight times, (M1L, K4) 31 times, (M1L, K5) eight times, M1L, K2. 256 sts.
Sizes 47.25" & 52.75": K2, (M1L, K3) 24 (8) times, (M1L, K4) 15 (47) times, (M1L, K3) 24 (8) times, M1L, K2. 272 (304) sts.
Size 55.75": K2, (M1L, K4) 63 times, M1L, K2. 320 sts.
Sizes 61.25" & 64": K2, (M1L, K5) 16 (24) times, (M1L, K4) 31 (15) times, (M1L, K5) 16 (24) times, M1L, K2. 352 (368) sts. 96 (104, 112, 128, 136)(152, 160, 176, 184) sts each for Front and Back.

Knit two rnds.
Begin Pine Cable from chart or written instructions. Rep Rnds 1–6 of pattern until body measures 16 (16, 16.5, 16.5, 16.5)(17, 17, 17.5, 17.5)" or desired body length as measured from underarm. End after an even pattern row.

Sizes – (36.25, -, -, 47.25)(52.75, -, -, 64)" Only
Remove BOR M, work an additional 4 sts as established, then replace M for new BOR.

Front
Armhole Shaping

Note: While decreasing for armholes/neckline, complete cable sts as established as available sts allow.
Row 1: BO 3 (5, 5, 8, 9)(12, 12, 15, 15) sts at underarm, work next row of Pine Cable to middle M; place next 96 (104, 112, 128, 136)(152, 160, 176, 184) sts on st holder or scrap yarn for Back, noting chart row worked. Turn to work flat.
Row 2 (WS): BO 3 (5, 5, 8, 9)(12, 12, 15, 15) sts at underarm, P to end of row (even row of Pine Cable). 90 (94, 102, 112, 118)(128, 136, 146, 154) sts.
Row 3 (RS): K1, SSK, work next RS row of Pine Cable until last 3 sts, K2tog, K1. 2 sts dec.
Row 4: P across.
Rep Rows 3–4 another 1 (3, 4, 6, 8)(10, 11, 13, 14) time(s). 86 (86, 92, 98, 100)(106, 112, 118, 124) sts.

WE until piece measures 7 (7, 7.5, 8, 8.5)(8.5, 9.5, 10, 10.5)" from underarm, ending after a RS row.

Neckline Shaping

Prepare a second ball of yarn; for the following rows, work both shoulders at the same time remembering to switch to the correct ball of yarn for each shoulder.
Row 1 (WS): P29 (29, 32, 34, 34)(37, 39, 41, 43), then place next 28 (28, 28, 30, 32)(32, 34, 36, 38) center sts on st holder or scrap yarn; using new ball of yarn, P29 (29, 32, 34, 34)(37, 39, 41, 43) to end.
Row 2 (RS): Work as established to last 3 sts, K2tog, K1, cont to next shoulder, K1, SSK, work to end. 2 sts dec, 1 at each side of neckline.
Row 3: P across both shoulders.
Rep Rows 2–3 another 5 (6, 6, 6, 6)(7, 7, 7, 7) times. 23 (22, 25, 27, 27)(29, 31, 33, 35) sts on each shoulder.

WE in pattern until total armhole depth measures 10 (10.5, 11, 11.5, 12)(12.5, 13.5, 14, 14.5)", ending on a WS row. Place remaining sts on st holders or scrap yarn.

Back

Armhole Shaping

Place the held 96 (104, 112, 128, 136)(152, 160, 176, 184) sts onto needles. Remember to start where you left off on Pine Cable pattern (it should be an odd row).
Row 1 (RS): BO 3 (5, 5, 8, 9)(12, 12, 15, 15) sts at underarm, work next row of Pine Cable as established to end.
Row 2 (WS): BO 3 (5, 5, 8, 9)(12, 12, 15, 15) sts at underarm, P to end. 90 (94, 102, 112, 118)(128, 136, 146, 154) sts.
Row 3: K1, SSK, work next RS row of Pine Cable until last 3 sts, K2tog, K1. 2 sts dec.
Row 4: P across.
Rep Rows 3–4 another 1 (3, 4, 6, 8)(10, 11, 13, 14) time(s). 86 (86, 92, 98, 100)(106, 112, 118, 124) sts.

WE as established until piece measures 8 (8.5, 9, 9, 9.5)(10, 10.5, 11, 11.5)" from underarm, ending on a RS row.

Neckline Shaping

Prepare a second ball of yarn; for the following rows, work both shoulders at the same time, remembering to switch to the correct ball of yarn for each shoulder.
Row 1 (WS): P27 (26, 29, 32, 32)(34, 37, 39, 41), then place the next 32 (34, 34, 34, 36)(38, 38, 40, 42) sts on st holder or scrap yarn; using new ball of yarn, P27 (26, 29, 32, 32)(34, 37, 39, 41) to end.
Row 2 (RS): Work as established to last 3 sts, K2tog, K1, cont to next shoulder, K1, SSK, work to end. 2 sts dec, 1 at each neckline edge.
Row 3: P across both shoulders.
Rep Rows 2–3 another 3 (3, 3, 4, 4)(4, 5, 5, 5) times. 23 (22, 25, 27, 27)(29, 31, 33, 35) sts on each shoulder.

WE in pattern until total armhole depth measures 10 (10.5, 11, 11.5, 12)(12.5, 13.5, 14, 14.5)", ending on a WS row.
Place right shoulder sts on st holder or scrap yarn.

Shoulder Seaming

Return the 23 (22, 25, 27, 27)(29, 31, 33, 35) sts from back left shoulder to needles. Work 3-Needle Bind Off to join left shoulder.
Rep for right shoulder.

Sleeves (make two the same)

Option 1: Stockinette Sleeves

PM at top of shoulder at seam; PM at bottom of armhole at underarm. Starting at underarm and using DPNs, PU and K 31 (33, 35, 37, 40)(42, 44, 46, 50) sts between Ms on each side, for a total of 62 (66, 70, 74, 80)(84, 88, 92, 100) sts. PM for BOR at underarm.
Use Top-Down Diagram as a guide. PM 11 (11, 12, 13, 14)(15, 17, 18, 21) sts from top M on both the left and right (M1 and M2). PM 1 st after armhole BO on each side (M3 and M4).

Short Rows

Start at BOR.
Short Row 1 (RS): K to M1, W&T.
Short Row 2 (WS): P to M2, W&T.
Short Row 3: K to wrapped st, K this st, working wrap tog with st, then W&T next st.
Short Row 4: P to wrapped st, P this st, working wrap tog with st, then W&T next st.
Rep Short Rows 3–4 until all sts have been worked before M3 and M4. After final rep of Row 4, K to BOR M. Remove M1 and M4.

Dec Rnds

Rnd 1: K all, hiding wraps from final short row.
Rnds 2–5 (5, 5, 5)(5, 5, 5, 4): Knit all.
Rnd 6 (6, 6, 6)(6, 6, 6, 5): K1, K2tog, K to last 3 sts, SSK, K1. 2 sts dec.
Rep all rnds another 10 (10, 10, 11, 13)(14, 16, 17, 20) times. 40 (44, 48, 50, 52)(54, 54, 56, 58) sts.

WE until sleeve measures approx 15.5 (16, 16.5, 17.5, 18)(18.5, 18.5, 19.75, 19.75)" from underarm, or 2" shorter than desired length.

Switch to smaller DPNs.
Work 1x1 Rib for 2", or until sleeve measures approx 17.5 (18, 18.5, 19.5, 20)(20.5, 20.5, 21.75, 21.75)".
BO loosely in Rib pattern, and weave in loose ends.

Option 2: Cabled Sleeves

PM at top of shoulder at seam; PM at bottom of armhole at underarm. Starting at underarm and using DPNs, PU and K 40 (40, 48, 48, 48)(56, 56, 56, 64) sts between Ms on each side, for a total of 80 (80, 96, 96, 96)(112, 112, 112, 128) sts. PM for BOR at underarm.
Use Top-Down Diagram as a guide. PM 13 (13, 16, 16, 16)(19, 19, 19, 21) sts from top M on both the left and right (M1 and M2). PM 1 st after armhole BO on each side (M3 and M4).

Short Rows

To prepare for short rows, center the cable design at top of sleeve (center of shoulder on diagram). You may choose whether to center between columns 8 and 9, or 1 and 16. Once you have decided, count backwards to M2 so you know which column to start chart on. Mark this column to remember where to start on Row 3 of short rows.
When working cables on arms, wait to work a cable until all 4 cable sts are available. Do not count the st just wrapped.
Short Row 1: K to M1, W&T.
Short Row 2: P to M2, W&T.
Short Row 3: Start Pine Cable at marked column to M1; K wrapped st, working wrap tog with st, then W&T next st.
Short Row 4: P to wrapped st, P this st, working wrap tog with st, then W&T next st.
Short Row 5: Work as established to wrapped st, K this st, working wrap tog with st, then W&T next st.
Rep Rows 4–5 until all sts have been worked before M3 and M4. End on a Row 4. After this last row, work as established to M3, then K remaining sts to BOR.

Dec Rnds

Rnd 1: K all, hiding wraps from final short row.
Rnd 2: Starting at M4, count back to BOR to determine which column to start at in Pine Cable. Work next odd row in pattern, where you left off when finishing short rows.
Rnds 3–12: Work Pine Cable as established.

Treeline Sweater

Dec Rnd: K2tog, K to last 2 sts, SSK. 2 sts dec.
Work Dec Rnd every 13 rnds 5 (5, 6, 6, 7)(7, 7, 7, 7) more times. 68 (68, 82, 82, 80)(96, 96, 96, 112) sts.

WE as established until sleeve measures approx 15.5 (16, 16.5, 17.5, 19)(19, 19, 19, 19.5)" from underarm, or 2" shorter than desired length. End on an odd pattern row.

On next rnd, dec by 26 (26, 34, 34, 30)(46, 46, 46, 56) sts evenly using the following instructions for size being made.
Sizes 33.5" & 36.25": K1, K2tog five times, (K2tog, K1) 15 times, K2tog six times. 42 sts.
Sizes 39" & 44.5": K1, K2tog ten times, (K2tog, K1) 13 times, K2tog eleven times. 48 sts.
Size 47.25": K1, K2tog five times, (K2tog, K1) 19 times, K2tog six times. 50 sts.
Size 52.75": K1, K2tog 21 times, (K2tog, K1) three times, K2tog 22 times. 50 sts.
Size 55.75" & 61.25": K1, K2tog 21 times, (K2tog, K1) three times, K2tog 21 times, K2tog. 50 sts.
Size 64": K2tog to end. 56 sts.

Work 1x1 Rib for 2" or until sleeve measures approx 17.5 (18, 18.5, 19.5, 21)(21, 21, 21, 21.5)".
BO loosely in Rib pattern, and weave in loose ends.

Neckline
With RS facing, place the 32 (34, 34, 34, 36)(38, 38, 40, 42) sts from back neck and 28 (28, 28, 30, 32)(32, 34, 36, 38) sts from front neck onto DPNs.

Starting at beginning of back neck sts, work as follows. (K3, K2tog) across back neck until last 2 (4, 4, 4, 1) (3, 3, 0, 2) sts then K; PU and K 4 (4, 4, 5, 5)(5, 6, 6, 6) sts before shoulder seam, PU and K 6 (7, 7, 7, 7)(8, 8, 8, 8) sts after shoulder seam.
Sizes 33.5–55.75": (K2tog, K3) across front neck until last 3 (3, 3, 0, 2) (2, 4, -, -) sts then K2tog and K remaining stitches.
Sizes 61.25" & 64": K2tog, (K2tog, K3) across remaining front neck until last (4, 5) sts, then K2tog and K remaining sts.
PU and K 6 (7, 7, 7, 7)(8, 8, 8, 8) sts before shoulder seam, PU and K 4 (4, 4, 5, 5)(5, 6, 6, 6) sts after shoulder seam.
PM for BOR.
68 (72, 72, 76, 780 (82, 86, 88, 92) sts for neckline.

Work 1x1 Rib for approx 1.25".
BO loosely in Rib pattern, and weave in loose ends.

Finishing
Weave in remaining ends, wash, and block to size.

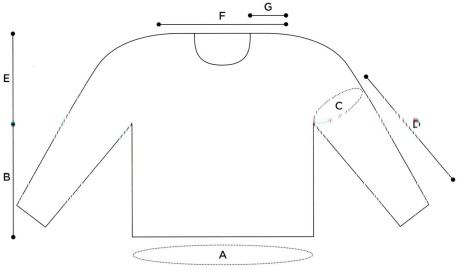

A chest circumference 33.5 (36.25, 39, 44.5, 47.25)(52.75, 55.75, 61.25, 64)"
B body length 16 (16, 16.5, 16.5, 16.5)(17, 17, 17.5, 17.5)"
C sleeve circumference (in St st) 13.75 (14.75, 15.5, 16.5, 17.75)(18.75, 19.5, 20.5, 22.25)"
C sleeve circumference (in cable pattern) 14 (14, 16.75, 16.75, 16.75)(19.5, 19.5, 19.5, 22.5)"
D sleeve length 17.5 (18, 18.5, 19.5, 20)(20.5, 20.5, 21.75, 21.75)"
E armhole depth 10 (10.5, 11, 11.5, 12)(12.5, 13.5, 14, 14.5)"
F shoulder width, across back 15 (15, 16, 17, 17.5)(18.5, 19.5, 20.5, 21.5)"
G single shoulder width 4 (3.75, 4.25, 4.75, 4.75)(5, 5.5, 5.75, 6)"

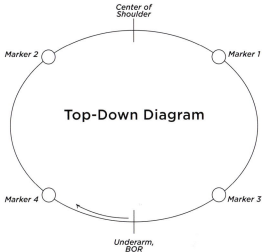

Pine Cable

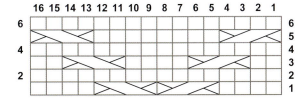

LEGEND

☐ **K**
RS: Knit stitch
WS: Purl stitch

2 over 2 Right Cable (2/2 RC)
Sl2 to CN, hold in back; K2, K2 from CN

2 over 2 Left Cable (2/2 LC)
Sl2 to CN, hold in front; K2, K2 from CN

Treeline Sweater

RAQUETTES SHAWL
by Karen Riehl

FINISHED MEASUREMENTS
23" width × 60" length

YARN
Stroll™ Tweed (fingering weight, 65% Fine Superwash Merino Wool, 25% Nylon, 10% Donegal Tweed; 231 yards/50g): Dill Heather 26292, 8 skeins

NEEDLES
US 7 (4.5mm) 24–32" circular needles, or size to obtain gauge

NOTIONS
Yarn Needle
Stitch Markers
Cable Needle
Blocking Pins and/or Wires

GAUGE
27 sts and 28 rows = 4" in Raquettes Pattern, blocked

For pattern support, contact hello@poppyspompom.com

Raquettes Shawl

Notes:

This shawl design was inspired by endless snow and the winter activities it brings. Although staying inside knitting during the winter months may be preferable, working this pattern might have you reminiscing about times snowshoeing through the freshly fallen snow.

The mock-lace cable border and bold dual cables surrounding lace add dimension and movement to the Raquettes Shawl. The 160-stitch wide pattern is worked over the length of the body, with the cables worked on the right side and the lace worked on the wrong side.

Charts are worked flat; read RS rows (odd numbers) from right to left, and WS rows (even numbers) from left to right.

MCL (Mock Cable Left)
The stitch pattern is worked over 3 sts from left to right.
Step 1: With RH needle tip, PU third st on LH needle.
Step 2: Pass this st over the 2 skipped sts, then drop the passed-over st.
Step 3: Work K1, YO, K1 with the 2 sts on LH needle.

MCR (Mock Cable Right)
Step 1: With RH needle tip, Sl 3 sts from LH needle to RH needle.
Step 2: With LH needle tip, PU front of the third st on RH needle, and pull it over the 2 sts to its left, then drop the passed-over st.
Step 3: With LH needle tip, move the 2 sts from RH needle back to LH needle.
Step 4: Work K1, YO, K1 with the 2 sts on LH needle.

2/2 LC (2 over 2 Left Cable)
Sl2 to CN, hold in front; K2, K2 from CN.

2/2 RC (2 over 2 Right Cable)
Sl2 to CN, hold in back; K2, K2 from CN.

2/1 RPC (2 over 1 Right Cable, Purl back)
Sl1 to CN and hold in back; K2, then P1 from CN.

2/1 LPC (2 over 1 Left Cable, Purl back)
Sl2 to CN and hold in front; P1, then K2 from CN.

Raquettes Pattern (flat over 160 sts)
Row 1 (RS): K2, P1, MCL, P10, *2/2 LC, SM, 2/2 RC, P3, K2, P1, K2, P8, SM, P8, K2, P1, K2, P3; rep from * two more times, 2/2 LC, SM, 2/2 RC, P10, MCL, P1, Sl2 WYIF.
Row 2 (WS): K3, P3, K10, *P8, K3, P2, K1, P2, (K2tog, YO) eight times, P2, K1, P2, K3; rep from * two more times, P8, K10, P3, K1, Sl2 WYIF.
Row 3: K2, P1, K3, P9, *2/1 RPC, 2/2 LC, 2/1 LPC, P2, (2/1 LPC) two times, P14, (2/1 RPC) two times, P2; rep from * two more times, 2/1 RPC, 2/2 LC, 2/1 LPC, P9, K3, P1, Sl2 WYIF.
Row 4: K3, P3, K9, *P2, K1, P4, K1, P2, K3, P2, K1, P2, (K2tog, YO) seven times, P2, K1, P2, K3; rep from * two more times, P2, K1, P4, K1, P2, K9, P3, K1, Sl2 WYIF.
Row 5: K2, P1, MCR, P8, *(2/1 RPC) two times, (2/1 LPC) two times, P2, (2/1 LPC) two times, P12, (2/1 RPC) two times, P2, (2/1 RPC) two times, (2/1 LPC) two times, P2, (2/1 LPC) two times, P12; rep from * three more times, (2/1 RPC) two times, P2, (2/1 RPC) two times (2/1 LPC) two times, P8, MCR, P1, Sl2 WYIF.
Row 6: K3, P3, K8, *P2, K1, P2, K2tog, YO, P2, K1, P2, K3, P2, K1, P2, (K2tog, YO) six times, P2, K1, P2, K3; rep from * four more times, P2, K1, P2, K2tog, YO, P2, K1, P2, K8, P3, K1, Sl2 WYIF.
Row 7: K2, P1, K3, P7, *(2/1 RPC) two times, P2, (2/1 LPC) two times, P2, (2/1 LPC) two times, P10; rep from * three more times, (2/1 RPC) two times, P2, (2/1 RPC) two times, P2, (2/1 LPC) two times, P7, K3, P1, Sl2 WYIF.
Row 8: K3, P3, K7, *P2, K1, P2, (K2tog, YO) two times, P2, K1, P2, K3, P2, K1, P2, (K2tog, YO) five times, P2, K1, P2, K3; rep from * four more times, P2, K1, P2, (K2tog, YO) two times, P2, K1, P2, K7, P3, K1, Sl2 WYIF.
Row 9: K2, P1, MCL, P6, *(2/1 RPC) two times, P4, (2/1 LPC) two times, P2, (2/1 LPC) two times, P8; rep from * three more times, (2/1 RPC) two times, P2, (2/1 RPC) two times, P4, (2/1 LPC) two times, P6, MCL, P1, Sl2 WYIF.
Row 10: K3, P3, K6, *P2, K1, P2, (K2tog, YO) three times, P2, K1, P2, K3, P2, K1, P2, (K2tog, YO) four times, P2, K1, P2, K3; rep from * four more times, P2, K1, P2, (K2tog, YO) three times, P2, K1, P2, K6, P3, K1, Sl2 WYIF.
Row 11: K2, P1, K3, P5, *(2/1 RPC) two times, P6, (2/1 LPC) two times, P2, (2/1 LPC) two times, P6, (2/1 RPC) two times, P2; rep from * five more times, (2/1 RPC) two times, P6, (2/1 LPC) two times, P5, K3, P1, Sl2 WYIF.
Row 12: K3, P3, K5, *P2, K1, P2, (K2tog, YO) four times, P2, K1, P2, K3, P2, K1, P2, (K2tog, YO) three times, P2, K1, P2, K3; rep from * four more times, P2, K1, P2, (K2tog, YO) four times, P2, K1, P2, K5, P3, K1, Sl2 WYIF.
Row 13: K2, P1, MCR, P4, *(2/1 RPC) two times, P8, (2/1 LPC) two times, P2, (2/1 LPC) two times, P4, (2/1 RPC) two times, P2; rep from * three more times, (2/1 RPC) two times, P8, 2/1 LPC two more times, P4, MCR, P1, Sl2 WYIF.
Row 14: K3, P3, K4, *P2, K1, P2, (K2tog, YO) five times, P2, K1, P2, K3, P2, K1, P2, (K2tog, YO) two times, P2, K1, P2, K3; rep from * four more times, P2, K1, P2, (K2tog, YO) five times, P2, K1, P2, K4, P3, K1, Sl2 WYIF.
Row 15: K2, P1, K3, P3, *(2/1 RPC) two times, P10, (2/1 LPC) two times, P2, (2/1 LPC) two times, P2; rep from * three more times, (2/1 RPC) two times, P2, (2/1 RPC) two times, P10, (2/1 LPC) two times, P3, K3, P1, Sl2 WYIF.
Row 16: K3, P3, K3, *P2, K1, P2, (K2tog, YO) six times, P2, K1, P2, K3, P2, K1, P2, K2tog, YO, P2, K1, P2, K3; rep from * two more times, P2, K1, P2, (K2tog, YO) six times, P2, K1, P2, K3, P3, K1, Sl2 WYIF.
Row 17: K2, P1, MCL, P2 *(2/1 RPC) two times, P12, (2/1 LPC) two times, P2, (2/1 LPC) two times, (2/1 RPC) two times, P2; rep from * two more times, (2/1 RPC) two times, P12, (2/1 LPC) two times, P2, MCL, P1, Sl2 WYIF.

Row 18: K3, P3, K2, *P2, K1, P2, (K2tog, YO) seven times, P2, K1, P2, K3, P2, K1, P4, K1, P2, K3; rep from * two more times, P2, K1, P2, (K2tog, YO) seven times, P2, K1, P2, K2, P3, K1, Sl2 WYIF.
Row 19: K2, P1, K3, P1 *(2/1 LPC) two times, P14, (2/1 LPC) two times, P2, 2/1 LPC, 2/2 LC, 2/1 RPC, P2; rep from * two more times, (2/1 RPC) two times, P14, (2/1 LPC) two times, P2, K3, P1, Sl2 WYIF.
Row 20: K3, P3, K1, *P2, K1, P2, (K2tog, YO) eight times, P2, K1, P2, K3, P8, K3; rep from * two more times, P2, K1, P2, (K2tog, YO) eight times, P2, K1, P2, K1, P3, K1, Sl2 WYIF.
Row 21: K2, P1, MCR, P1 *K2, P1, K2, P16, K2, P1, K2, P3, 2/2 RC, 2/2 LC, P3; rep from * two more times, K2, P1, K2, P16, K2, P1, K2, P1, MCR, P1, Sl2 WYIF.
Row 22: K3, P3, K1, *P2, K1, P2, (K2tog, YO) eight times, P2, K1, P2, K3, P8, K3; rep from * two more times, P2, K1, P2, (K2tog, YO) eight times, P2, K1, P2, K1, P3, K1, Sl2 WYIF.
Row 23: K2, P1, K3, P1 *K2, P1, K2, P16, K2, P1, K2, P2, 2/1 RPC, K4, 2/1 LPC, P2; rep from * two more times, K2, P1, K2, P16, K2, P1, K2, P1, K3, P1, Sl2 WYIF.
Row 24: K3, P3, K1, *P2, K1, P2, (K2tog, YO) eight times, P2, K1, P2, K2, P2, K1, P4, K1, P2, K2; rep from * two more times, P2, K1, P2, (K2tog, YO) eight times, P2, K1, P2, K1, P3, K1, Sl2 WYIF.
Row 25: K2, P1, MCL, P1, *(2/1 LPC) two times, P14, (2/1 RPC) two times, P1, (2/1 RPC) two times, (2/1 LPC) two times, P1; rep from * two more times, P1, (2/1 LPC) two times, P12, (2/1 RPC) two times, P2, MCL, P1, Sl2 WYIF.
Row 26: K3, P3, K2, *P2, K1, P2 (K2tog, YO) seven times, P2, K1, P2, K2, P2, K1, P2, K2tog, YO, P2, K1, P2, K2, P2, K1; rep from * two more times, P2, K1, P2 (K2tog, YO) seven times, P2, K1, P2, K2, P3, K1, Sl2 WYIF.
Row 27: K2, P1, K3, P2, *(2/1 LPC) two times, P12, (2/1 RPC) two times, P1, (2/1 RPC) two times, P2, (2/1 LPC) two times, P1; rep from * two more times, P1, (2/1 LPC) two times, P10, (2/1 RPC) two times, P3, K3 Sl2 WYIF.
Row 28: K3, P3, K3, *P2, K1, P2 (K2tog, YO) six times, P2, K1, P2, K2, P2, K1, P2, (K2tog, YO) two times, P2, K1, P2, K2; rep from * three more times, (K2tog, YO) six times, P2, K3, P3, K1, Sl2 WYIF.
Row 29: K2, P1, M3R, P3, *(2/1 LPC) two times, P10, (2/1 RPC) two times, P1, (2/1 RPC) two times, P4, (2/1 LPC) two times, P1; rep from * two more times, P1, (2/1 LPC) two times, P8, (2/1 RPC) two times, P3, M3R, P1, Sl2 WYIF.
Row 30: K3, P3, K4, *P2, K1, P2 (K2tog, YO) five times, P2, K1, P2, K2, P2, K1, P2, (K2tog, YO) three times, P2, K1, P2, K2; rep from * three more times, (K2tog, YO) five times, P2, K4, P3, K1, Sl2 WYIF.
Row 31: K2, P1, K3, P4, *(2/1 LPC) two times, P8, (2/1 RPC) two times, P1, (2/1 RPC) two times, P6, (2/1 LPC) two times, P1; rep from * two more times, P1, (2/1 LPC) two times, P8, (2/1 RPC) two times, P4, K3, P1, Sl2 WYIF.
Row 32: K3, P3, K5, *P2, K1, P2 (K2tog, YO) four times, P2, K1, P2, K2, P2, K1, P2, (K2tog, YO) four times, P2, K1, P2, K2; rep from * three more times, (K2tog, YO) four times, P2, K5, P3, K1, Sl2 WYIF.
Row 33: K2, P1, MCL, P5, *(2/1 LPC) two times, P6, (2/1 RPC) two times, P1, (2/1 RPC) two times, P8, (2/1 LPC) two times, P1; rep from * two more times, P1, (2/1 LPC) two times, P8, (2/1 RPC) two times, P5, MCL, P1, Sl2 WYIF.
Row 34: K3, P3, K6, *P2, K1, P2 (K2tog, YO) three times, P2, K1, P2, K2, P2, K1, P2, (K2tog, YO) five times, P2, K1, P2, K2; rep from * three more times, (K2tog, YO) three times, P2, K6, P3, K1, Sl2 WYIF.
Row 35: K2, P1, K3, P6, *(2/1 LPC) two times, P4, (2/1 RPC) two times, P1, (2/1 RPC) two times, P10, (2/1 LPC) two times, P1; rep from * two more times, P1, (2/1 LPC) two times, P8, (2/1 RPC) two times, P6, K3, P1, Sl2 WYIF.
Row 36: K3, P3, K7, *P2, K1, P2, (K2tog, YO) two times, P2, K1, P2, K2, P2, K1, P2, (K2tog, YO) six times, P2, K1, P2, K2; rep from * three more times, (K2tog, YO) two times, P2, K7, P3, K1, Sl2 WYIF.
Row 37: K2, P1, MCR, P7, *(2/1 LPC) two times, P2, (2/1 RPC) two times, P1, (2/1 RPC) two times, P12, (2/1 LPC) two times, P1; rep from * two more times, P1, (2/1 LPC) two times, P8, (2/1 RPC) two times, P7, MCR, P1, Sl2 WYIF.
Row 38: K3, P3, K8, *P2, K1, P2, K2tog, YO, P2, K1, P2, K2, P2, K1, P2, (K2tog, YO) seven times, P2, K1, P2, K2; rep from * three more times, K2tog, YO, P2, K8, P3, K1, Sl2 WYIF.
Row 39: K2, P1, K3, P8, *(2/1 LPC) two times, (2/1 RPC) two times, P1, (2/1 RPC) two times, P14, (2/1 LPC) two times, P1; rep from * two more times, P1, (2/1 LPC) two times, P8, (2/1 RPC) two times, P8, K3, P1, Sl2 WYIF.
Row 40: K3, P3, K9, *P2, K1, P4, K1, P2, K2, P2, K1, P2, (K2tog, YO) eight times, P2, K1, P2, K2; rep from * three more times, P2, K9, P3, K1, Sl2 WYIF.
Row 41: K2, P1, MCL, P9, *2/1 LPC, 2/2 LC, 2/1 RPC, P1, (2/1 RPC) two times, P16, (2/1 LPC) two times, P1; rep from * two more times, P1, (2/1 LPC) two times, P8, (2/1 RPC) two times, P9, MCL, P1, Sl2 WYIF.
Row 42: K3, P3, K10, *P8, K3, P2, K1, P2, (K2tog, YO) eight times, P2, K1, P2, K3; rep from * three more times, P2, K10, P3, K1, Sl2 WYIF.
Rep Rows 1–42 for pattern.

DIRECTIONS

CO 160 sts, and PM every 20 sts to better track cable locations. (M locations are given as SM in the first row of the written pattern instructions to ensure proper placement.)

Work Raquettes Pattern from chart or written instructions, completing Rows 1–42.

Rep Rows 1–42 nine more times, working the mock lace cable edging as established, every fourth row throughout (so MLC sts will be worked on Rows 3, 7, and so on for the next rep, then back to Rows 1, 5, and so on for the third rep).

BO on the final Row 42 rep.

Finishing
Weave in ends, wash, and block to dimensions.

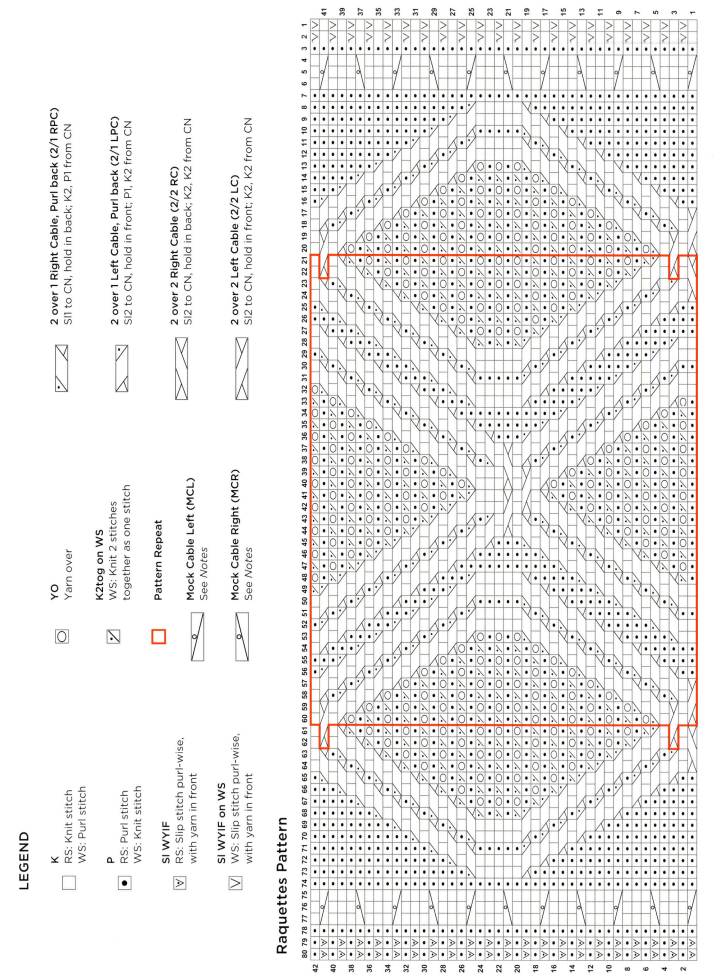

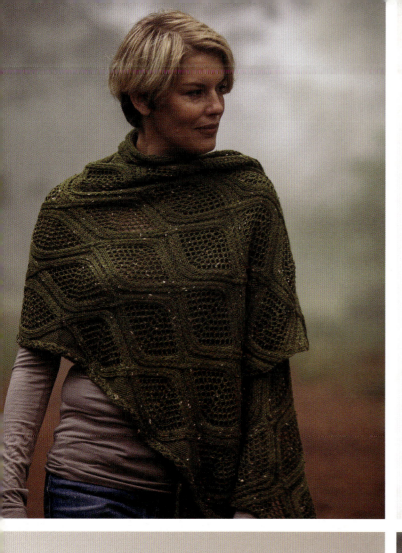

ANTRIM CARDIGAN
by Jill Wright

FINISHED MEASUREMENTS
38 (41.5, 46, 49.5, 54)(57.5, 62, 65.5, 70)" finished chest circumference; meant to be worn with 6" positive ease
Sample is 41.5" size; models are 35"

YARN
Woodland Tweed™ (Aran/heavy worsted weight, 80% Merino Wool, 15% Baby Alpaca, 5% Viscose; 180 yards/100g): Bare 27614, 7 (8, 9, 10, 11)(12, 13, 14, 15) hanks

NEEDLES
US 9 (5.5mm) straight or circular needles (24" or longer), or size to obtain gauge

NOTIONS
Yarn Needle
Locking Stitch Markers
Cable Needle
Scrap Yarn or Stitch Holders
Nine Buttons, 1" in diameter
Sewing Needle and Thread
Blocking Pins and/or Wires

GAUGE
38 sts and 16 rows = 6.5" × 2.75" in Antrim Cable Panel, blocked
24 sts and 24 rows = 4" in Cable Rib Stitch, blocked
18 sts and 24 rows = 4" in Double Moss Stitch, blocked
25 sts and 24 rows = 4" in 1x1 Rib, blocked

For pattern support, contact jill2who@gmail.com

Antrim Cardigan

Notes:

Cozy, comfortable, and casual perfectly describe the beautiful counties in Ireland with their winding pathways and stunning scenery. These deceptively simple cables ebb and flow like the wandering streams searching for the Irish Sea.

This drop shoulder Antrim Cardigan has simple lines allowing the cables to shine. The flow of the Cabled Rib into the main cable panels may look complex, but the stitch pattern is easily remembered. Don't forget the buttonholes!

Charts are worked flat; read RS rows (odd numbers) from right to left, and WS rows (even numbers) from left to right.

2/1 LPC (2 over 1 Left Cable, Purl back)
Sl2 to CN, hold in front; P1, K2 from CN.

2/1 RPC (2 over 1 Right Cable, Purl back)
Sl1 to CN, hold in back; K2, P1 from CN.

2/2 LC (2 over 2 Left Cable)
Sl2 to CN, hold in front; K2, K2 from CN.

2/2 RC (2 over 2 Right Cable)
Sl2 to CN, hold in back; K2, K2 from CN.

2/2 LPC (2 over 2 Left Cable, Purl back)
Sl2 to CN, hold in front; P2, K2 from CN.

2/2 RPC (2 over 2 Right Cable, Purl back)
Sl2 to CN, hold in back; K2, P2 from CN.

1x1 Rib Button Band (flat over 8 sts)
All Rows: (K1, P1) four times.

Cable Rib Stitch (flat over a multiple of 8 sts)
Row 1 (RS): (P1, K2, P1) to end.
Row 2 (WS): (K1, P2, K1) to end.
Rows 3-6: Rep Rows 1-2.
Row 7: (P1, 2/1 LPC, 2/1 RPC, P1) to end.
Row 8: (K2, P4, K2) to end.
Row 9: (P2, 2/2 LC, P2) to end.
Row 10: (K2, P4, K2) to end.
Row 11: (P1, 2/1 RPC, 2/1 LPC, P1) to end.
Row 12: (K1, P2, K1) to end.
Row 13: (P1, K2, P1) to end.
Rows 14-17: Rep Rows 12-13 two more times.
Row 18: (K1, P2, K1) to end.
Row 19: (2/1 RPC, P2, 2/1 LPC) to end.
Row 20: (P2, K4, P2) to end.
Rep Rows 1-20 for pattern.

Double Moss Stitch (flat over an even number of sts)
Row 1 (RS): (K1, P1) to end.
Row 2 (WS): Rep Row 1.
Row 3: (P1, K1) to end.
Row 4: Rep Row 3.
Rep Rows 1-4 for pattern.

Double Moss Stitch (flat over an odd number of sts)
Row 1 (RS): (K1, P1) to last st, K1.
Row 2 (WS): (P1, K1) to last st, P1.
Row 3: Rep Row 2.
Row 4: Rep Row 1.
Rep Rows 1-4 for pattern.

Antrim Cable Pattern (flat over 38 sts)
Row 1 (RS): P1, 2/2 LC, (P4, 2/2 RC) four times, P1.
Row 2 (WS): K1, P4, (K4, P4) four times, K1.
Row 3: P1, K4, P3, 2/1 RPC, (2/2 LPC, 2/2 RPC) two times, 2/1 LPC, P3, K4, P1.
Row 4: K1, P4, K3, P2, (K3, P4, K1) two times, K2, P2, K3, P4, K1.
Row 5: P1, 2/2 LC, P2, 2/1 RPC, (P3, 2/2 LC, P1) two times, P2, 2/1 LPC, P2, 2/2 RC, P1.
Row 6: K1, P4, K2, (P2, K4, P2) three times, K2, P4, K1.
Row 7: P1, K2, (K2, P2) two times, P1, 2/1 RPC, 2/2 LPC, 2/2 RPC, 2/1 LPC, P1, (P2, K2) two times, K2, P1.
Row 8: K1, P4, K2, * P2, (K3, P2) two times ; rep from * once more, K2, P4, K1.
Row 9: P1, 2/2 LC, P2, (K2, P3) two times, 2/2 RC, (P3, K2) two times, P2, 2/2 RC, P1.
Row 10: K1, P4, K2, * P2, (K3, P2) two times ; rep from * once more, K2, P4, K1.
Row 11: P1, K2, (K2, P2) two times, P1, 2/1 LPC, 2/2 RPC, 2/2 LPC, 2/1 RPC, P1, (P2, K2) two times, K2, P1.
Row 12: K1, P4, K2, (P2, K4, P2) three times, K2, P4, K1.
Row 13: P1, 2/2 LC, P2, 2/1 LPC, (P3, 2/2 LC, P1) two times, P2, 2/1 RPC, P2, 2/2 RC, P1.
Row 14: K1, P4, K3, P2, (K3, P4, K1) two times, K2, P2, K3, P4, K1.
Row 15: P1, K4, P3, 2/1 LPC, (2/2 RPC, 2/2 LPC) two times, 2/1 RPC, P3, K4, P1.
Row 16: K1, P4, (K4, P4) four times, K1.
Rep Rows 1-16 for pattern

DIRECTIONS

Back

Loosely CO 104 (114, 122, 132, 140)(150, 158, 168, 176) sts.
Row 1 (RS): Work Row 1 of Cable Rib Stitch beginning with st 1 (8, 4, 7, 7)(2, 2, 5, 5) of chart, End after completing a st 8 (1, 5, 2, 2)(7, 7, 4, 4).
Row 2 (WS): Work Row 2 of Cable Rib Stitch making sure to work 2x2 Rib as established in Row 1.
Cont as established until 19 rows of chart have been worked. On Row 20 of pattern work as follows.

Sizes 36, (-, 46, -, 54)(-, 62, -, 70)" Only
Row 20 (WS): Work 52 (-, 61, -, 70)(-, 79, -, 88) sts in pattern as established, M1 in next st, work across remaining sts in pattern as established. 105 (-, 123, -, 141)(-, 159, -, 177 sts).

Sizes - (41.5, -, 49.5, -)(57.5, -, 65.5, -)" Only
Row 20 (WS): Work - (56, -, 65, -)(74, -, 83, -) sts in pattern as established, K2tog, work across remaining sts in pattern as established. - (113, -, 131, -)(149, -, 167, -) sts.

Body (resume all sizes)
Row 1 (RS): Work 5 (6, 10, 15, 15)(20, 20, 25, 25) sts in Row 1 of Double Moss Stitch corresponding with odd or even numbers as stated, work Row 1 of Antrim Cable Pattern, work 19 (25, 27, 25, 35)(33, 43, 41, 51) sts in Row 1 of Double Moss Stitch (odd numbers only), work Row 1 of Antrim Cable Pattern, work 5 (6, 10, 15, 15)(20, 20, 25, 25) sts in Row 1 of Double Moss Stitch corresponding with odd or even numbers as stated.

Cont as established until work measures 18 (18, 18, 18, 18)(17, 17, 17, 17)" from CO edge. PM at each end of last row worked. Cont as established until work measures 25 (26, 26, 27, 27)(27, 27, 28, 28)" from CO edge.

Shoulder Shaping
Rows 1-2: Work as established and BO 12 (13, 14, 15, 17)(17, 19, 19, 21) sts at beginning of each row.
Rows 3-4: Work as established and BO 12 (12, 14, 15, 16)(17, 18, 19, 21) sts at beginning of each row.
Rows 5-6: Work as established and BO 11 (12, 14, 14, 16)(16, 18, 19, 20) sts at beginning of each row.
Sl remaining 35 (39, 39, 43, 43)(49, 49, 53, 53) sts to st holder or scrap yarn for collar.

Front
Right Front Rib
Loosely CO 55 (59, 64, 68, 73)(77, 82, 86, 91) sts.
Row 1 (RS): Work 8 sts in 1x1 Rib Button Band, work Row 1 of Cable Rib Stitch beginning with st 2 (7, 6, 7, 2)(3, 6, 7, 2) to end, ending after completing a st 8 (1, 5, 2, 2)(7, 7, 4, 4).
Rows 2-4: Cont in pattern as established.
Row 5 (Buttonhole Row): K1, P1, K1, YO, K2tog, P1, K1, P1, work to end as established.
Cont in pattern as established, working all 20 rows of Cable Rib Stitch.

Moving forward, work buttonhole in band on RS row every 20 rows.

Right Front Body
Row 1 (RS): Work 8-st button band, work 4 (7, 8, 7, 12)(11, 16, 15, 20) sts of Row 1 in Double Moss Stitch corresponding with odd or even numbers as stated, work Row 1 of Antrim Cable Pattern, work 5 (6, 10, 15, 15)(20, 20, 25, 25) sts of Row 1 in Double Moss Stitch corresponding with odd or even numbers as stated.

Cont in pattern as established until work measures 18 (18, 18, 18, 18)(17, 17, 17, 17)" from CO edge. With RS facing, PM at left edge of last row worked to mark armhole.
Cont in pattern as established until work measures 23 (24, 24, 25, 25)(25, 25, 26, 26)" from CO edge, ending with a WS row.

Right Neck Shaping
Setup Row (RS): Work as established for 12 (12, 12, 14, 14)(17, 17, 20, 20) sts, Sl these worked sts to scrap yarn or st holder, work to end.
Dec Row 1 (WS): Work to last 2 sts, K2tog. 1 st dec.
Dec Row 2 (RS): SSK, work to end. 1 st dec.
Rep Dec Rows 1-2 another 3 (4, 4, 4, 4)(4, 4, 3, 3) times.
Rep Dec Row 1 - (-, -, -, -)(-, -, 1, 1) more time. 35 (37, 42, 44, 49)(50, 55, 57, 62) sts.
WE for 4 (2, 2, 2, 2)(2, 2, 3, 3) more rows.

Shoulder Shaping
Row 1 (WS): BO 12 (13, 14, 15, 17)(17, 19, 19, 21) sts, work to end.
Row 2 (RS): WE as established.
Row 3: BO 12 (12, 14, 15, 16)(17, 18, 19, 21) sts, work to end.
Row 4: WE as established.
Row 5: BO remaining sts.

Left Front Rib
Loosely CO 55 (59, 64, 68, 73)(77, 82, 86, 91) sts.
Row 1 (RS): Work Row 1 of Cable Rib Stitch beginning with st 1 (8, 4, 7, 7)(2, 2, 5, 5), ending after completing a st 7 (2, 3, 2, 7)(6, 3, 2, 7); work 8-st button band to end.
Cont in pattern as established until all rows of chart have been worked.

Left Front Body
Row 1 (RS): Work 5 (6, 10, 15, 15)(20, 20, 25, 25) sts in Double Moss Stitch corresponding with odd or even numbers as stated, work Row 1 of Antrim Cable Pattern, work 4 (7, 8, 7, 12)(11, 16, 15, 20) sts in Double Moss Stitch corresponding with odd or even numbers as stated, (P1, K1) four times.

Cont in pattern as established until work measures 18 (18, 18, 18, 18)(17, 17, 17, 17)" from CO edge. With RS facing, PM at right edge of last row worked to mark armhole.
Cont in pattern as established until work measures 23 (24, 24, 25, 25)(25, 25, 26, 26)" from CO edge, ending with a WS row.

Left Neck Shaping
Setup Row (RS): Work as established to last 12 (12, 12, 14, 14)(17, 17, 20, 20) sts, Sl these remaining unworked sts to scrap yarn or st holder, turn.
Dec Row 1 (WS): SSK, work as established to end. 1 st dec.
Dec Row 2 (RS): Work to last 2 sts, K2tog. 1 st dec.
Rep Dec Rows 1-2 another 3 (4, 4, 4, 4)(4, 4, 3, 3) times.
Rep Dec Row 1 - (-, -, -, -)(-, -, 1, 1) more time. 35 (37, 42, 44, 49)(50, 55, 57, 62) sts.
WE for 5 (3, 3, 3, 3)(3, 3, 4, 4) more rows.

Shoulder Shaping
Row 1 (RS): BO 12 (13, 14, 15, 17)(17, 19, 19, 21) sts, work to end.
Row 2 (WS): WE as established.
Row 3: BO 12 (12, 14, 15, 16)(17, 18, 19, 21) sts, work to end.
Row 4: WE as established
Row 5: BO remaining sts.

Sleeves (make two the same)
Cuff
Loosely CO 44 (44, 44, 50, 50)(52, 52, 56, 56) sts.
Row 1 (RS): Work Row 1 of Cable Rib Stitch beginning with st 3 (3, 3, 8, 8)(6, 6, 5, 5); end after completing a st 6 (6, 6, 3, 3)(1, 1, 4, 4).
Cont in pattern as established until all rows of chart have been worked.

Sleeve Body

Row 1 (RS): KFB in first st, work next 2 (2, 2, 5, 5)(6, 6, 8, 8) sts in Double Moss Stitch corresponding with odd or even numbers as stated, work Row 1 of Antrim Cable Pattern, work 2 (2, 2, 5, 5)(6, 6, 8, 8) sts in Double Moss Stitch corresponding with odd or even numbers as stated, KFB in last st. 2 sts inc.

WE as established for 5 (3, 3, 3, 2)(2, 2, 1, 1) row(s).
Inc Row: KFB, work to last st, KFB. 2 sts inc.
Rep last 6 (4, 4, 4, 3)(3, 3, 2, 2) rows until there are 80 (88, 88, 98, 98)(106, 106, 128, 128) sts.

Sleeve Length — Women's/Shorter

WE as established for 1 (15, 9, 1, 10)(4, 4, 7, 1) more row(s), ending with a WS row.
BO all sts.

Sleeve Length — Men's/Longer

WE as established for 7 (27, 27, 19, 34)(30, 28, 33, 31) more rows, ending with a WS row.
BO all sts.

Finishing

Wash, and block pieces to diagram. Rib may be left unstretched if a closer fit is desired.
Sew shoulder seams. Sew sleeves to body between Ms. Sew side and sleeve seams.

Collar

Sizes 38 (41.5, 46, -, -)(-, -, -, -)" Only
Setup Row (RS): With RS facing, beginning at right front neck, Sl sts from st holder and work across 12 sts as established, PU and K 10 (11, 11, -, -)(-, -, -, -) sts up right side neck, K1(3, 3, -, -)(-, -, -, -), (KFB, K1) 17 times, K0 (1, 1, -, -)(-, -, -, -), PU and K 10 (11, 11, -, -)(-, -, -, -) sts down left side neck, Sl sts from holder onto needle, work to end as established. 96 (102, 102, -, -)(-, -, -, -) sts.

Sizes - (-, -, 49.5, 54)(-, -, -, -)" Only
Setup Row (RS): With RS facing, beginning at right front neck, Sl sts from st holder and work across 14 sts as established, PU and K 15 sts up right side neck, K3, (KFB, K1) five times, (K1, KFB) seven times, K2, (K1, KFB) five times, K3, PU and K 15 sts down left side neck, Sl sts from holder onto needle, work to end as established. 110 sts.

Sizes - (-, -, -, -)(57.5, 62, -, -)" Only
Setup Row (RS): With RS facing, beginning at right front neck, Sl sts from st holder and work across 17 sts as established, PU and K 21 sts up right side neck, K4, (KFB, K1) three times, (K1, KFB) three times, K4, (KFB, K1) five times, (K1, KFB) three times, K4, (KFB, K1) three times, K3, PU and K 21 sts down left side neck, Sl 17 sts from holder onto needle, work to end as established. 122 sts.

Sizes - (-, -, -, -)(-, -, 65.5, 70)" Only
Setup Row (RS): With RS facing, beginning at right front neck, Sl sts from st holder and work across 20 sts as established, PU and K 28 sts up right side neck, K2, (KFB, K2) 17 times, PU and K 28 sts down left side neck, Sl 20 sts from st holder onto needle, work to end as established. 132 sts.

Resume All Sizes

Setup Row (WS): Work 8 sts as established, then work Row 2 of Cable Rib Stitch beginning with st 8 (3, 3, 3, 3)(1, 1, 2, 2) working across to last 8 sts, ending after completing a st 1 (6, 6, 6, 6)(8, 8, 7, 7), work last 8 sts as established.

Cont in pattern as established, working buttonhole in next RS row of right front band and ending with Row 12 of Cable Rib Stitch.
Next Row (RS): K1, P1, K1, YO, K2tog, P1, K1, P1, work to end.
Work three more rows as established.
BO in Cable Rib Stitch.

Using sewing needle and matching thread, sew buttons in place on left front band corresponding with buttonholes on right front band.
Weave in all ends.
Gently block collar if desired.

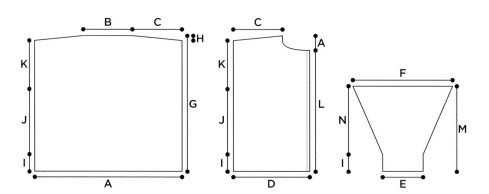

- **A** *back hem* 19.5 (21.25, 23.5, 25.25, 27.5)(29.25, 31.5, 33.25, 35.5)"
- **B** *back neck* 7 (8, 8, 8.75, 9.25)(10, 10.5, 11.25, 11.75)"
- **C** *shoulder* 6.25 (6.75, 7.75, 8.25, 9.25)(9.5, 10.5, 11, 12)"
- **D** *front* 10.25 (11.25, 12.25, 13.25, 14.25)(15.25, 16.25, 17.25, 18.25)"
- **E** *cuff* 7.25 (7.25, 7.25, 8.25, 8.25)(8.75, 8.75, 9.25, 9.25)"
- **F** *upper arm* 15.75 (17.5, 17.5, 19.75, 19.75)(21.5, 21.5, 26.5, 26.5)"
- **G** *nape to hem* 26 (27, 27, 28, 28)(28, 28, 29, 29)"
- **H** *shoulder rise* 1"
- **I** *rib/cuff* 3.5"
- **J** *body (top of rib to armhole)* 14.5 (14.5, 14.5, 14.5, 14.5)(13.5, 13.5, 13.5, 13.5)"
- **K** *armhole* 7 (8, 8, 9, 9)(10, 10, 11, 11)"
- **L** *front (hem to neck shaping)* 23 (24, 24, 25, 25)(25, 25, 26, 26)"
- **M** *women sleeve length (full)* 21.75 (20.75, 19.75, 19.75, 18.75)(17.75, 17.75, 16.75, 15.75)"
- **N** *women sleeve length (minus cuff)* 18.25 (17.25, 16.25, 16.25, 15.25)(14.25, 14.25, 13.25, 12.25)"
- **M** *men sleeve length (full)* 22.75 (22.75, 22.75, 22.75, 22.75)(22.25, 21.75, 21.25, 20.75)"
- **N** *men sleeve length (minus cuff)* 19.25 (19.25, 19.25, 19.25, 19.25)(18.75, 18.75, 17.75, 17.25)"

LEGEND

☐ **K**
RS: Knit stitch
WS: Purl stitch

• **P**
RS: Purl stitch
WS: Knit stitch

2 over 1 Right Cable, Purl back (2/1 RPC)
Sl1 to CN, hold in back; K2, P1 from CN

2 over 1 Left Cable, Purl back (2/1 LPC)
Sl2 to CN, hold in front; P1, K2 from CN

2 over 2 Right Cable (2/2 RC)
Sl2 to CN, hold in back; K2, K2 from CN

2 over 2 Left Cable (2/2 LC)
Sl2 to CN, hold in front; K2, K2 from CN

2 over 2 Right Cable, Purl back (2/2 RPC)
Sl2 to CN, hold in back; K2, P2 from CN

2 over 2 Left Cable, Purl back (2/2 LPC)
Sl2 to CN, hold in front; P2, K2 from CN

Cable Rib Stitch

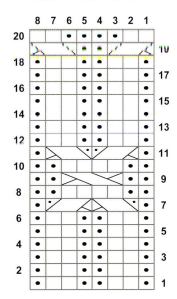

Double Moss Stitch

Antrim Cable Pattern

Antrim Full Chart

FIR BOUGH HAT
by Emily Kintigh

FINISHED MEASUREMENTS
18.5 (20.25, 22)″ finished circumference × 7.75 (8.5, 9.25)″ height; meant to be worn with approx 1–2″ negative ease
Sample is 20.25″ size

YARN
City Tweed™ (DK weight, 55% Merino Wool, 25% Superfine Alpaca, 20% Donegal Tweed; 123 yards/50g): Toad 24978, 2 (2, 3) balls

NEEDLES
US 6 (4mm) 16″ and 32″ circular needles for Magic Loop technique or DPNs, or size to obtain gauge
US 4 (3.5mm) DPNs or 16″ circular needles, or two sizes smaller than size used to obtain gauge

NOTIONS
Yarn Needle
Stitch Markers
Cable Needle

GAUGE
38 sts and 32 rnds = 4″ in Fir Bough Cable Pattern in the round, blocked

For pattern support, contact auntieemsstudio@gmail.com

Fir Bough Hat

Notes:

Inspired by the forests of the Pacific Northwest, the beautiful cables on the Fir Bough Hat resemble entwining tree trunks and branches. Even the decreases mimic trees as the "branches" become smaller and smaller near the top.

The hat is worked in the round starting from the 1x1 Rib, brim up. The decreases are worked into the cable pattern.

Charts are repeated 11 (12, 13) times across each round. Place markers between repeats if desired.

Charts are worked in the round; read each chart row from right to left as a RS row.

M1P (Make 1 Purl-wise)
Inserting LH needle from front to back, pick up the horizontal strand between the st just worked and the next st, and purl through the back loop.

2/2 LC (2 over 2 Left Cable)
Sl2 to CN, hold in front; K2, K2 from CN.

2/2 RC (2 over 2 Right Cable)
Sl2 to CN, hold in back; K2, K2 from CN.

2/2 LPC (2 over 2 Left Cable, Purl back)
Sl2 to CN, hold in front; P2, K2 from CN.

2/2 RPC (2 over 2 Right Cable, Purl back)
Sl2 to CN, hold in back; K2, P2 from CN.

2/1 LPC (2 over 1 Left Cable, Purl back)
Sl2 to CN, hold in front; P1, K2 from CN.

2/1 RPC (2 over 1 Right Cable, Purl back)
Sl1 to CN, hold in back; K2, P1 from CN.

LPT (Left Twist, Purl back)
Sl1 to CN, hold in front; P1, K1 from CN.

RT (Right Twist)
Sl1 to CN, hold in back; K1, K1 from CN.

RPT (Right Twist, Purl back)
Sl1 to CN, hold in back; K1, P1 from CN.

Fir Bough Cable (in the round over a multiple of 16 sts)
Rnd 1: 2/2 LC, P8, 2/2 RC.
Rnd 2: K4, P8, K4.
Rnd 3: K2, 2/2 LPC, P4, 2/2 RPC, K2.
Rnd 4: K2, P2, K2, P4, K2, P2, K2.
Rnd 5: K2, P2, 2/2 LPC, 2/2 RPC, P2, K2.
Rnd 6: K2, P4, K4, P4, K2.
Rnd 7: K2, P4, 2/2 RC, P4, K2,
Rnd 8: Rep Rnd 6.
Rnd 9: K2, P2, 2/2 RPC, 2/2 LPC, P2, K2.
Rnd 10: Rep Rnd 4.
Rnd 11: K2, 2/2 RPC, P4, 2/2 LPC, K2.
Rnd 12: Rep Rnd 2.
Rep Rnds 1–12 for pattern.

Crown (in the round beginning with a multiple of 16 sts)
Rnd 1: K1, SSK, K1, P8, K1, K2tog, K1. 2 sts dec (each rep).
Rnd 2: 2/2 LC, P6, 2/2 RC.
Rnd 3: K1, P1, K1, SSK, P4, K2tog, K1, P1, K1. 2 sts dec.
Rnd 4: K1, P1, 2/1 LPC, P2, 2/1 RPC, P1, K1.
Rnd 5: K1, P2, K1, SSK, K2tog, K1, P2, K1. 2 sts dec.
Rnd 6: K1, P2, 2/2 RC, P2, K1.
Rnd 7: K1, P2, K4, P2, K1.
Rnd 8: K1, P1, 2/1 RPC, 2/1 LPC, P1, K1.
Rnd 9: K1, K2tog, K1, P2, K1, SSK, K1. 2 sts dec.
Rnd 10: SSK, K1, P2, K1, K2tog. 2 sts dec.
Rnd 11: LPT, P2, RPT.
Rnd 12: P1, SSK, K2tog, P1. 2 sts dec.
Rnd 13: P1, RT, P1.
Rnd 14: RPT, LPT.
Rnd 15: K1, P2, K1.
Rnd 16: Rep Rnd 15.
Rnd 17: SSK, K2tog. 2 sts dec.
Rnd 18: K2tog. 1 st dec.

DIRECTIONS

Brim
With smaller needles, loosely CO 110 (120, 130) sts. Join to work in the rnd, being careful not to twist sts; PM for BOR. Work 1x1 Rib until piece measures 1" from CO edge.

Body
Switch to larger 16" needles.

Sizes 18.5 (-, 22)" Only
Setup Rnd: *K3, M1L, (P1, M1P) four times, K1, M1L, K2; rep from * to end. 176 (-, 208) sts.
Begin working Fir Bough Cable from chart or written instructions. Work Rnds 1–12 of pattern 3 (-, 4) times.
Cont to Crown.

Size - (20.25, -)" Only
Setup Rnd: *K1, M1L, (P1, M1P) two times, K1, M1L, K2, (P1, M1P) two times, K2; rep from * to end. - (192, -) sts.
Begin working Fir Bough Cable from chart or written instructions, working Rnds 7–12 first, then Rnds 1–12 of pattern three times.
Cont to Crown.

Crown
Switch to 32" circular needles for Magic Loop technique or DPNs when sts no longer fit comfortably on 16" needles. Work Rnds 1–18 of Crown from chart or written instructions. 11 (12, 13) sts.
Next Rnd: (K2tog) 5 (6, 6) times, K1 (0, 1). 6 (6, 7) sts.
Break yarn and pull through remaining sts.

Finishing
Weave in ends, wash, and block to measurements.

LEGEND

- **No Stitch** — Placeholder—no stitch made
- **Knit Stitch**
- **Purl Stitch**
- **K2tog** — Knit 2 stitches together as one stitch
- **SSK** — Slip, slip, knit slipped stitches together
- **Right Twist (RT)** — Sl1 to CN, hold in back; K1, K1 from CN
- **Right Twist, Purl back (RPT)** — Sl1 to CN, hold in back; K1, P1 from CN
- **Left Twist, Purl back (LPT)** — Sl1 to CN, hold in front; P1, K1 from CN
- **2 over 1 Right Cable, Purl back (2/1 RPC)** — Sl1 to CN, hold in back; K2, P1 from CN
- **2 over 1 Left Cable, Purl back (2/1 LPC)** — Sl2 to CN, hold in front; P1, K2 from CN
- **2 over 2 Right Cable (2/2 RC)** — Sl2 to CN, hold in back; K2, K2 from CN
- **2 over 2 Left Cable (2/2 LC)** — Sl2 to CN, hold in front; K2, K2 from CN
- **2 over 2 Right Cable, Purl back (2/2 RPC)** — Sl2 to CN, hold in back; K2, P2 from CN
- **2 over 2 Left Cable, Purl back (2/2 LPC)** — Sl2 to CN, hold in front; P2, K2 from CN

Fir Bough Cable

Crown

Fir Bough Hat 81

ROOTS JUMPER
by Helen Metcalfe

FINISHED MEASUREMENTS
33.5 (37.75, 41.25, 45.25, 49.5, 53.75) (57.75, 61.25, 65.5, 69.75, 73.25)" finished chest circumference; meant to be worn with 6-8" positive ease
Sample is 37.75" size; models are 35"

YARN
Wool of the Andes™ (sport weight, 100% Peruvian Highland Wool; 137 yards/50g): Pampas Heather 25653, 12 (13, 14, 15, 16, 17)(19, 20, 21, 22, 23) skeins if using women's/shorter sleeve instructions; 13 (14, 16, 17, 18, 19)(21, 22, 23, 24, 25) skeins if using men's/longer sleeve instructions

NEEDLES
US 4 (3.5mm) straight or circular needles (24" or longer), or size to obtain gauge
US 3 (3.25mm) straight or circular needles (24" or longer), plus DPNs or two 24" circular needles for two circulars technique, or one size smaller than size used to obtain gauge

NOTIONS
Yarn Needle
Cable Needle
Stitch Marker (1)
Stitch Holders (2) or Scrap Yarn
Blocking Pins and/or Wires

GAUGE
27 sts and 32 rows = 4" in Chart A Pattern, blocked

For pattern support, contact hmetcalfe@hotmail.co.uk

Roots Jumper

Notes:
Panels of twisted stitches emulate the texture of tree roots that twist and entwine toward the neckline in a cable pattern that can be found on the front and back.

Roots Jumper is worked in four separate pieces, each from the bottom up. The neckband is picked up and worked in 1x1 Rib to finish. The garment is unisex and two sleeve lengths are given for each size.

Charts are worked flat; read RS rows (odd numbers) from right to left, and WS rows (even numbers) from left to right.

RT (Right Twist)
Sl1 to CN, hold in back; K1, K1 from CN.

2/1 LPT (2 over 1 Left Twist, Purl back, with RT)
Sl2 to CN, hold in front; P1, work RT from CN.

2/1 RPT (2 over 1 Right Twist, Purl back, with RT)
Sl1 to CN, hold in back; work RT, P1 from CN.

2/1/2 LPC (2 over 2 Left Cable, Purl 1 center back, with RTs)
Sl3 to CN, hold in front; work RT, Sl left-most st from CN back to LH needle and P it; work RT from CN.

2/1/2 RPC (2 over 2 Right Cable, Purl 1 center back, with RTs)
Sl3 to CN, hold in back; work RT, Sl left-most st from CN back to LH needle and P it; work RT from CN.

Chart A (flat over a multiple of 5 sts plus 3)
Row 1 (RS): P3, (RT, P3) to end.
Row 2 (WS): (K3, P2) to last 3 sts, K3.
Rep Rows 1–2 for pattern.

Chart B (flat over a multiple of 27 sts)
Row 1 (RS): RT, (P3, 2/1 LPT, P1, 2/1 RPT) two times, P3, RT.
Row 2 (WS): P2, K4, P2, K1, P2, K5, P2, K1, P2, K4, P2.
Row 3: RT, P4, 2/1/2 LPC, P5, 2/1/2 RPC, P4, RT.
Row 4: Rep Row 2.
Row 5: RT, (P3, 2/1 RPT, P1, 2/1 LPT) two times, P3, RT.
Row 6: (P2, K3) five times, P2.
Row 7: (RT, P3) five times, RT.
Row 8: Rep Row 6.
Row 9: 2/1 LPT, P1, 2/1 RPT, (P3, RT) two times, P3, 2/1 LPT, P1, 2/1 RPT.
Row 10: (K1, P2) two times, K4, P2, K3, P2, K4, (P2, K1) two times.
Row 11: P1, 2/1/2 RPC, P4, RT, P3, RT, P4, 2/1/2 LPC, P1.
Row 12: Rep Row 10.
Row 13: 2/1 RPT, P1, 2/1 LPT, (P3, RT) two times, P3, 2/1 RPT, P1, 2/1 LPT.
Row 14–16: Rep Rows 6–8.
Rep Rows 1–16 for pattern.

Chart C (flat over a multiple of 7 sts)
Row 1 (RS): 2/1 LPT, P1, 2/1 RPT.
Row 2 (WS): (K1, P2) two times, K1.
Row 3: P1, 2/1/2 LPC, P1.
Row 4: Rep Row 2.
Row 5: 2/1 RPT, P1, 2/1 LPT.
Row 6: P2, K3, P2.
Row 7: RT, P3, RT.
Row 8: Rep Row 6.
Rep Rows 1–8 for pattern.

Chart D (flat over a multiple of 7 sts)
Row 1 (RS): 2/1 LPT, P1, 2/1 RPT.
Row 2 (WS): (K1, P2) two times, K1.
Row 3: P1, 2/1/2 RPC, P1.
Row 4: Rep Row 2.
Row 5: 2/1 RPT, P1, 2/1 LPT.
Row 6: P2, K3, P2.
Row 7: RT, P3, RT.
Row 8: Rep Row 6.
Rep Rows 1–8 for pattern.

DIRECTIONS

Back
**Using larger needles, CO 115 (129, 141, 155, 169, 183)(195, 209, 223, 237, 249) sts.
Row 1 (RS): P1 (3, 4, 1, 3, 0)(1, 3, 0, 2, 3), rep Row 1 of Chart A from chart or written instructions until 1 (3, 4, 1, 3, 0)(1, 3, 0, 2, 3) sts remain, P to end.
Row 2 (WS): K1 (3, 4, 1, 3, 0)(1, 3, 0, 2, 3), rep Row 2 of Chart A until 1 (3, 4, 1, 3, 0)(1, 3, 0, 2, 3) sts remain, K to end.
Cont as established until Back measures 11.5 (11.5, 12.5, 12.5, 13.5, 15.5)(15.5, 16.5, 16.5, 17.5, 17.5)", ending after a WS row.

Next Row (RS): Work as established for 44 (51, 57, 64, 71, 78)(84, 91, 98, 105, 111) sts, work Row 1 of Chart B from chart or written instructions, work as established to end.
Rep last row until Rows 1–16 of Chart B have been completed, followed by Rows 1–8.

Next Row (RS): Work as established for 34 (41, 47, 54, 61, 68)(74, 81, 88, 95, 101) sts, work Row 1 of Chart C from chart or written instructions, P3, work Row 9 of Chart B, P3, work Row 1 of Chart D from chart or written instructions, work as established to end.
Next Row (WS): Work as established for 34 (41, 47, 54, 61, 68)(74, 81, 88, 95, 101) sts, work Row 2 of Chart D, K3, work Row 10 of Chart B, K3, work Row 2 of Chart C, work as established to end.
Cont as established for six more rows until a full rep of the Charts have been completed.

Next Row (RS): Work as established for 29 (36, 42, 49, 56, 63)(69, 76, 83, 90, 96) sts, (work Row 9 of Chart B, P3) two times, work as established to end.
Next Row (WS): Work as established for 29 (36, 42, 49, 56, 63)(69, 76, 83, 90, 96) sts, (work Row 10 of Chart B, K3) two times, work as established to end.
Cont as established for six more rows. Cont to work Chart B as set until Rows 1–8 are complete.

Next Row (RS): Work as established for 14 (21, 27, 34, 41, 48) (54, 61, 68, 75, 81) sts, (work Row 1 of Chart B, P3) three times, work as established to end.
Next Row (WS): Work as established for 14 (21, 27, 34, 41, 48) (54, 61, 68, 75, 81) sts, (work Row 2 of Chart B, K3) three times, work as established to end.**

Cont to rep Chart B as established until Back measures 24 (24, 25, 25, 26, 28)(28, 29, 29, 30, 30)", ending after Chart Row 4.

Working as established, BO 5 (6, 6, 7, 8, 9)(10, 11, 12, 13, 14) sts at beginning of next 12 (12, 4, 6, 4, 6)(6, 6, 4, 6, 6) rows. 55 (57, 117, 113, 137, 129)(135, 143, 175, 159, 165) sts.
Working as established, BO - (-, 7, 8, 9, 10)(11, 12, 13, 14, 15) sts at beginning of next - (-, 8, 6, 8, 6)(6, 6, 8, 6, 6) rows. 55 (57, 61, 65, 65, 69)(69, 71, 71, 75, 75) sts.
Place remaining sts on st holder.

Front
Work as for Back from ** to **. 115 (129, 141, 155, 169, 183) (195, 209, 223, 237, 249) sts.
Cont to rep Chart B as established until Front measures 21.5 (21.5, 22.5, 22.5, 23.5, 25.5)(25.5, 26.5, 26.5, 27.5, 27.5)", ending after Chart Row 16.

Cont to follow Chart A and Chart B to end as established while working shaping AT THE SAME TIME. When Chart B is interrupted by the shaping, revert to Chart A.
Next Row (RS): Work 49 (55, 59, 64, 71, 76)(82, 88, 95, 100, 106) sts as established, turn, cont on working these sts only. Place remaining 66 (74, 82, 91, 98, 107)(113, 121, 128, 137, 143) unworked sts on st holder.

Cont as established and BO 4 sts at beginning of next two WS rows. 41 (47, 51, 56, 63, 68)(74, 80, 87, 92, 98) sts.
Cont as established and BO 3 sts at beginning of next WS row. 38 (44, 48, 53, 60, 65)(71, 77, 84, 89, 95) sts.
Cont as established and BO 2 sts at beginning of next WS row. 36 (42, 46, 51, 58, 63)(69, 75, 82, 87, 93) sts.

Next Row (RS): Work as established to last 3 sts, K2tog, K1. 1 st dec.
Next Row (WS): WE as established.
Rep the last two rows five more times. 30 (36, 40, 45, 52, 57)(63, 69, 76, 81, 87) sts.

Cont as established and BO 5 (6, 6, 7, 8, 9)(10, 11, 12, 13, 14) sts at beginning of next 6 (6, 2, 3, 2, 3)(3, 3, 2, 3, 3) RS rows, then BO - (-, 7, 8, 9, 10)(11, 12, 13, 14, 15) sts at beginning of next - (-, 4, 3, 4, 3)(3, 3, 4, 3, 3) RS rows. All sts have been bound off.

With RS facing, leave center 17 (19, 23, 27, 27, 31)(31, 33, 33, 37, 37) sts on st holder and place 49 (55, 59, 64, 71, 76)(82, 88, 95, 100, 106) sts back onto larger needles.

Cont as established and BO 4 sts at beginning of next two RS rows. 41 (47, 51, 56, 63, 68)(74, 80, 87, 92, 98) sts.
Cont as established and BO 3 sts at beginning of next RS row. 38 (44, 48, 53, 60, 65)(71, 77, 84, 89, 95) sts.

Cont as established and BO 2 sts at beginning of next RS row. 36 (42, 46, 51, 58, 63)(69, 75, 82, 87, 93) sts.

WE for one WS row.
Next Row (RS): K1, SSK, work as established to end. 1 st dec.
Rep the last two rows five more times. 30 (36, 40, 45, 52, 57)(63, 69, 76, 81, 87) sts.
WE for two rows.

Cont as established and BO 5 (6, 6, 7, 8, 9)(10, 11, 12, 13, 14) sts at beginning of next 6 (6, 2, 3, 2, 3)(3, 3, 2, 3, 3) WS rows, then BO - (-, 7, 8, 9, 10)(11, 12, 13, 14, 15) sts at beginning of next - (-, 4, 3, 4, 3)(3, 3, 4, 3, 3) WS rows. All sts have been bound off.

Women's/Shorter Sleeves (make two the same)
As sleeve shaping progresses, incorporate new sts into Chart A pattern as established.
**Using larger needles, CO 57 (57, 62, 65, 68, 73)(73, 75, 75, 78, 78) sts.
Row 1 (RS): P2 (2, 2, 1, 0, 0)(0, 1, 1, 0, 0), rep Row 1 of Chart A from chart or written instructions until 2 (2, 2, 1, 0, 0)(0, 1, 1, 0, 0) sts remain, P to end.
Row 2 (WS): K2 (2, 2, 1, 0, 0)(0, 1, 1, 0, 0), rep Row 2 of Chart A until 2 (2, 2, 1, 0, 0)(0, 1, 1, 0, 0) sts remain, K to end.
Rep Rows 1–2 seven more times.**

Inc Row (RS): P1, M1, work as established to last st, M1, P1. 2 sts inc.
Work 5 (5, 5, 3, 3, 3)(3, 3, 3, 3, 3) rows without shaping, as established.
Rep the last 6 (6, 6, 4, 4, 4)(4, 4, 4, 4, 4) rows 12 (6, 6, 27, 29, 25)(17, 16, 13, 11, 8) more times. 83 (71, 76, 121, 128, 125) (109, 109, 103, 102, 96) sts.

Sizes 33.5 (37.75, 41.25, -, -, 53.75)(57.25, 61.25, 65.5, 69.75, 73.25)" Only
Inc Row (RS): P1, M1, work as established to last st, M1, P1. 2 sts inc.
Work 3 (3, 3, -, -, 1)(1, 1, 1, 1, 1) rows without shaping, as established.
Rep the last 4 (4, 4, -, -, 2)(2, 2, 2, 2, 2) rows 8 (18, 18, -, -, 4) (16, 19, 25, 29, 35) more times. 101 (109, 114, -, -, 135)(143, 149, 155, 162, 168) sts.

Resume All Sizes
Work 10 (6, 6, 12, 4, 10)(10, 8, 8, 8, 8) rows without shaping, as established.
BO remaining sts.

Men's/Longer Sleeves (make two the same)
Work as for Women's/Shorter Sleeve from ** to **.
Inc Row (RS): P1, M1, work as established to last st, M1, P1. 2 sts inc.
Work 7 (5, 5, 5, 5, 5)(5, 5, 3, 3, 3) rows without shaping, as established.
Rep the last 8 (6, 6, 6, 6, 6)(6, 6, 4, 4, 4) rows 10 (25, 25, 21, 18, 17)(9, 4, 39, 34, 32) more times. 79 (109, 114, 109, 106, 109)(93, 85, 155, 148, 144) sts.

Sizes 33.5 (-, -, 45.25, 49.5, 53.75)(57.25, 61.25, -, 69.75, 73.25)" Only

Inc Row (RS): P1, M1, work as established to last st, M1, P1. 2 sts inc.

Work 5 (-, -, 3, 3, 3)(3, 3, -, 1, 1) rows without shaping, as established.

Rep the last 6 (-, -, 4, 4, 4)(4, 4, -, 2, 2) rows 10 (-, -, 5, 10, 12)(24, 31, -, 6, 11) more times. 101 (-, -, 121, 128, 135)(143, 149, -, 162, 168) sts.

Resume All Sizes

WE for 14 (12, 12, 12, 10, 8)(8, 10, 8, 14, 12) rows without shaping, as established.

BO remaining sts.

Neckband

Seam shoulders.

With RS facing and smaller needles, PU and K 33 sts down left front neckline, K17 (19, 23, 27, 27, 31)(31, 33, 33, 37, 37) sts from front st holder, PU and K 33 sts up right front neckline, K55 (57, 61, 65, 65, 69)(69, 71, 71, 75, 75) from back st holder; PM to mark BOR. 138 (142, 150, 158, 158, 166)(166, 170, 170, 178, 178) sts.

Starting with a K st, work 1x1 Rib until Neckband measures 1". BO loosely in pattern.

Finishing

Weave in ends, wash, and block to diagram.

Line up the center of the top of the sleeve with the shoulder seam, sew tog using Mattress Stitch. Rep for other sleeve. Sew sleeve and side seams.

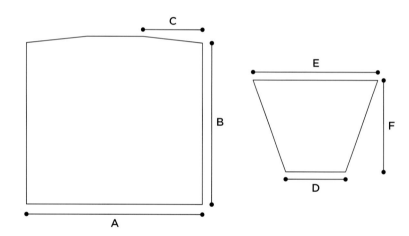

- **A** *body width* 17 (19, 21, 23, 25, 27)(29, 31, 33, 35, 37)"
- **B** *shoulder to hem* 24 (24, 25, 25, 26, 28)(28, 29, 29, 30, 30)"
- **C** *shoulder width* 4.5 (5.5, 6, 6.75, 7.75, 8.25)(9.25, 10.25, 11.25, 12, 13)"
- **D** *wrist* 8.5 (8.5, 9.25, 9.5, 10, 10.75)(10.75, 11, 11, 11.5, 11.5)"
- **E** *arm width at top* 15 (16.25, 17, 18, 19, 20)(21.25, 22, 23, 24, 25)"
- **F** *women's/shorter sleeve length* 17.5 (17.5, 17.5, 17.5, 17.5, 17.5)(16.5, 16.5, 16.5, 16.5, 16.5)"
- **F** *men's/longer sleeve length* 23"

LEGEND

- ☐ **K**
  RS: Knit stitch
  WS: Purl stitch

- ● **P**
  RS: Purl stitch
  WS: Knit stitch

- ▭ **Pattern Repeat**

Right Twist (RT)
Sl1 to CN, hold in back; K1, K1 from CN

2 over 1 Right Twist, Purl back, with RT (2/1 RPT)
Sl1 to CN, hold in back; work RT, P1 from CN

2 over 1 Left Twist, Purl back, with RT (2/1 LPT)
Sl2 to CN, hold in front; P1, work RT from CN

2 over 2 Left Cable, Purl 1 center back, with RTs (2/1/2 LPC)
Sl3 to CN, hold in front, work RT, Sl left-most st from CN back to left-hand needle and purl it; work RT from CN

2 over 2 Right Cable, Purl 1 center back, with RTs (2/1/2 RPC)
Sl3 to CN, hold in back; work RT, Sl left-most st from CN back to left-hand needle and purl it; work RT from CN

Chart A

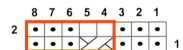

Chart B

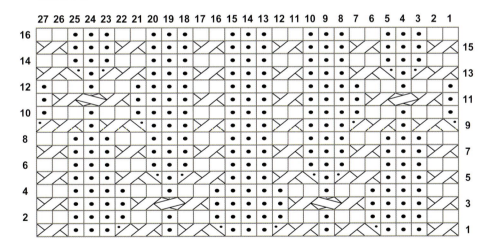

Chart C

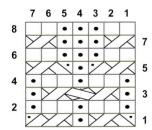

Chart D

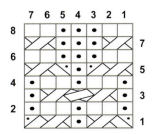

COUNTRY CROSSROADS SCARF
by Tina Spencer

FINISHED MEASUREMENTS
7.25" width × 70.5" length

YARN
City Tweed™ (DK weight, 55% Merino Wool, 25% Superfine Alpaca, 20% Donegal Tweed; 123 yards/50g): Habanero 24546, 6 balls

NEEDLES
US 5 (3.75mm) straight or DPNs, or size needed to obtain gauge

NOTIONS
Yarn Needle
Cable Needle
Blocking Pins and/or Wires
Stitch Markers (optional)

GAUGE
32 sts and 34 rows = 4" in Crossroads Pattern, blocked (gauge is not crucial, but it will affect finished size and yardage requirements)

For pattern support, contact youphoriabytina@gmail.com

Country Crossroads Scarf

Notes:
The Country Crossroads Scarf is meant to invoke memories of driving down backcountry roads in the fall, taking in the beautiful golden aspens while choosing the next road you want to explore.

The scarf is knit in stripes of knit and purl stitches, with groups of smaller and larger cables set up in diamond formations. The larger cables give the illusion of a big design block but actually break down into smaller "roads" that come together and cross over each other and then turn back into their respective small "roads" again.

Chart is worked flat and starts with a wrong side row; read RS rows (even numbers) from right to left, and WS rows (odd numbers) from left to right.

3/1/3 RPC (3 over 3 with 1 in center Right Purl Cable)
Sl4 to CN, hold in back; K3, then P1, K3 from CN.

3/1/3 LPC (3 over 3 with 1 in center Left Purl Cable)
Sl3 to CN, hold in front; K3, P1, then K3 from CN.

2/2 RC (2 over 2 Right Cable)
Sl2 to CN, hold in back; K2, then K2 from CN.

2/2 LC (2 over 2 Left Cable)
Sl2 to CN, hold in front; K2, then K2 from CN.

Crossroads Pattern (flat over 57 sts)
Row 1 (WS): P3, K3, P8, K3, (P3, K1) five times, P3, K3, P8, K3, P3.
Row 2 (RS): K3, P3, K8, P3, (K3, P1) five times, K3, P3, K8, P3, K3.
Row 3: Rep Row 1.
Row 4: P6, K8, P3, (K3, P1) five times, K3, P3, K8, P6.
Row 5: Rep Row 1.
Row 6: K3, P3, K2, 2/2 RC, K2, P3, (K3, P1) five times, K3, P3, K2, 2/2 RC, K2, P3, K3.
Row 7: Rep Row 1.
Row 8: P6, (2/2 LC) two times, P3, (K3, P1) two times, 3/1/3 RPC, (P1, K3) two times, P3, (2/2 LC) two times, P6.
Rows 9-11: Rep Rows 5-7.
Row 12: P6, (2/2 LC) two times, P3, K3, (P1, 3/1/3 LPC) two times, P1, K3, P3, (2/2 LC) two times, P6.
Rows 13-15: Rep Rows 5-7.
Row 16: P6, K8, P3, (3/1/3 RPC, P1) three times, P2, K8, P6.
Rows 17-19: Rep Rows 1-3.
Row 20: P6, K8, P3, K3, (P1, 3/1/3 LPC) two times, P1, K3, P3, K8, P6.
Row 21-23: Rep Rows 1-3.
Row 24: P6, K8, P3, (K3, P1) two times, 3/1/3 RPC, (P1, K3) two times, P3, K8, P6.
Rows 25-27: Rep Rows 5-7.
Row 28: P6, (2/2 LC) two times, P3, (K3, P1) five times, K3, P3, (2/2 LC) two times, P6.
Row 29: Rep Row 1.
Rows 30-33: Rep Rows 26-29.
Row 34-35: Rep Rows 6-7.
Row 36: Rep Row 24.
Rows 37-40: Rep Rows 17-20.
Rows 41-43: Rep Rows 1-3.
Row 44-45: Rep Rows 16-17.
Row 46-47: Rep Row 6-7.
Row 48: Rep Row 12.
Row 49-51: Rep Rows 5-7.
Row 52: Rep Row 8.
Row 53-55: Rep Rows 5-7.
Row 56: Rep Row 4.
Rows 57-60: Rep Rows 1-4.
Rep Rows 1-60 for pattern.

DIRECTIONS

CO 57 sts.

Work entire Crossroads Pattern from chart or written instructions.
Rep Rows 1-60 of pattern nine more times.

BO in pattern.

Finishing
Weave in all ends, wash, and block.
When blocking, be careful not to stretch the cables to prevent flattening. Optionally, the ribbing can be stretched out more to give a more visual definition between the knit and purl stitches.

Country Crossroad Chart

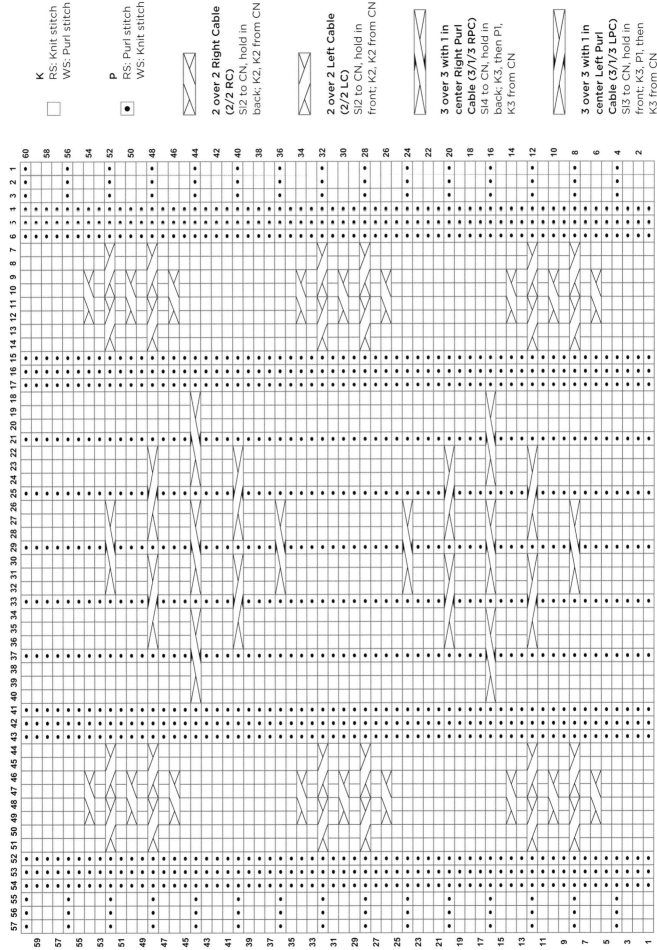

Country Crossroads Scarf

SLALOM PULLOVER
by Anni Howard

FINISHED MEASUREMENTS
36 (39.5, 43, 46.75, 52)(55.5, 61, 64.5, 68)" finished chest circumference; meant to be worn with 3.5–5" positive ease
Samples are 36" (brown) & 39.5" (gray); models are 35" except short-haired male model is 38"

YARN
Wool of the Andes™ Tweed (worsted weight, 80% Peruvian Highland Wool, 20% Donegal Tweed; 110 yards/50g): Sarsaparilla Heather 28308, 11 (13, 15, 16, 17)(18, 19, 20, 22) skeins
or Wool of the Andes™ (worsted weight, 100% Peruvian Highland Wool; 110 yards/50g): Crane Heather 28290, 11 (13, 15, 16, 17)(18, 19, 20, 22) skeins

NEEDLES
US 8 (5mm) straight needles, or size to obtain gauge

NOTIONS
Cable Needle
Yarn Needle
Stitch Holders (2) or Scrap Yarn

GAUGE
18 sts and 31 rows = 4" in Moss Stitch, blocked
20 sts and 30 rows = 4" in Rib, blocked
Panel Chart (58 stitches) measures 10" wide, blocked

For pattern support, contact anniknit@gmail.com

Slalom Pullover

Notes:

Perfect for après ski activities or for any day when you'd rather be out on the mountain slopes, this pullover includes cable panels inspired by ski tracks in the snow.

The body and sleeves are knitted flat and seamed. After 2x2 Rib and a narrow Reverse Stockinette Stitch band, the front features a textured Moss Stitch pattern at each side and a cable panel at the center. Both back and sleeves are knitted in Moss Stitch. The double neckband begins with a narrow band of Reverse Stockinette Stitch before being completed by 2x2 Rib.

When breaking off yarn at the end of knitting at shoulders and at top of sleeve, leave a long enough tail to sew up seams.

Charts are worked flat; read each RS row from right to left, and each WS row from left to right.

M1P (Make 1 Purl-wise)
Inserting LH needle from front to back, PU the horizontal strand between the st just worked and the next st, and P TBL.

RT (Right Twist, worked without a cable needle)
K into front of second st on LH needle then K first st; Sl both sts off needle tog.

LT (Left Twist, worked without a cable needle)
K into back of the second st on LH needle then K first st; Sl both sts off needle tog.

RPT (Right Twist over Purl, worked without a cable needle)
K into front of second st on LH needle then P first st; Sl both sts off needle tog.

LPT (Left Twist over Purl, worked without a cable needle)
P into back of second st on LH needle then K first st; Sl both sts off needle tog.

2/1 RPC (2 over 1 Right Cable, Purl back)
Sl1 to CN, hold in back; K2, P1 from CN.

2/1 LPC (2 over 1 Left Cable, Purl back)
Sl2 to CN, hold in front; P1, K2 from CN.

Cable Panel (flat over 58 sts)
Row 1 (RS): P7, (RPT, P1, RPT, P3) two times, 2/1 RPC, P2, RT, P2, 2/1 LPC, (P3, LPT, P1, LPT) two times, P7.
Row 2 (WS): K7, (P1, K2, P1, K4) two times, (P2, K3) two times, P2, (K4, P1, K2, P1) two times, K7.
Row 3: P6, (RPT, P1, RPT, P3) two times, 2/1 RPC, P2, RT, LT, P2, 2/1 LPC, (P3, LPT, P1, LPT) two times, P6.
Row 4: K6, (P1, K2, P1, K4) two times, P2, K3, P4, K3, P2, (K4, P1, K2, P1) two times, K6.
Row 5: P5, (RPT, P1, RPT, P3) two times, 2/1 RPC, P3, K4, P3, 2/1 LPC, (P3, LPT, P1, LPT) two times, P5.
Row 6: K5, (P1, K2, P1, K4) two times, P2, K4, P4, K4, P2, (K4, P1, K2, P1) two times, K5.
Row 7: P4, (RPT, P1, RPT, P3) two times, 2/1 RPC, P4, K4, P4, 2/1 LPC, (P3, LPT, P1, LPT) two times, P4.
Row 8: (K4, P1, K2, P1) two times, K4, P2, K5, P4, K5, P2, (K4, P1, K2, P1) two times, K4.
Row 9: (P3, RPT, P1, RPT) two times, P3, 2/1 RPC, P5, LPT, RPT, P5, 2/1 LPC, (P3, LPT, P1, LPT) two times, P3.
Row 10: K3, (P1, K2, P1, K4) two times, (P2, K7) two times, P2, (K4, P1, K2, P1) two times, K3.
Row 11: P2, (RPT, P1, RPT, P3) two times, 2/1 RPC, P7, RT, P7, 2/1 LPC, (P3, LPT, P1, LPT) two times, P2.
Row 12: K2, (P1, K2, P1, K4) two times, (P2, K8) two times, P2, (K4, P1, K2, P1) two times, K2.
Row 13: P2, (LPT, P1, LPT, P3) two times, 2/1 LPC, P7, RT, P7, 2/1 RPC, (P3, RPT, P1, RPT) two times, P2.
Row 14: Rep Row 10.
Row 15: (P3, LPT, P1, LPT) two times, P3, 2/1 LPC, P5, RT, LT, P5, 2/1 RPC, (P3, RPT, P1, RPT) two times, P3.
Row 16: Rep Row 8.
Row 17: P4, (LPT, P1, LPT, P3) two times, 2/1 LPC, P4, K4, P4, 2/1 RPC, (P3, RPT, P1, RPT) two times, P4.
Row 18: Rep Row 6.
Row 19: P5, (LPT, P1, LPT, P3) two times, 2/1 LPC, P3, K4, P3, 2/1 RPC, (P3, RPT, P1, RPT) two times, P5.
Row 20: Rep Row 4.
Row 21: P6, (LPT, P1, LPT, P3) two times, 2/1 LPC, P2, LPT, RPT, P2, 2/1 RPC, (P3, RPT, P1, RPT) two times, P6.
Row 22: Rep Row 2.
Row 23: P7, (LPT, P1, LPT, P3) two times, 2/1 LPC, P2, RT, P2, 2/1 RPC, (P3, RPT, P1, RPT) two times, P7.
Row 24: K8, (P1, K2, P1, K4) two times, (P2, K2) two times, P2, (K4, P1, K2, P1) two times, K8.
Rep Rows 1-24 for pattern.

Moss Stitch (flat over a multiple of 2 sts plus 1)
Row 1 (RS): (K1, P1) to last st, K1.
Row 2 (WS): P across.
Row 3: (P1, K1) to last st, P1.
Row 4: P across.
Rep Rows 1-4 for pattern.

DIRECTIONS

Front
CO 82 (90, 98, 106, 118)(126, 138, 146, 154) sts.
Row 1 (RS): (K2, P2) to last 2 sts, K2.
Row 2 (WS): (P2, K2) to last 2 sts, P2.
Cont in Rib as established for 3", ending after Row 2.

Next Row (RS): K across.
Beginning with a K row, work five rows in Rev St st.
Next Row (RS): K across.

Inc Row (WS): P27 (31, 35, 39, 45)(49, 55, 59, 63), M1P, P2, M1P, P4, M1P, P2, M1P, P3, M1P, P1, M1P, P2, M1P, P3, M1P, P1, M1P, P3, M1P, P2, M1P, P4, M1P, P2, M1P, P to last st, M1P, P1. 96 (104, 112, 120, 132)(140, 152, 160, 168) sts.

Body

Row 1 (RS): (K1, P1) 9 (11, 13, 15, 18)(20, 23, 25, 27) times, K1, work Row 1 of Cable Panel from chart or written instructions, (K1, P1) 9 (11, 13, 15, 18)(20, 23, 25, 27) times, K1.
Row 2 (WS): P19 (23, 27, 31, 37)(41, 47, 51, 55), work Row 2 of Cable Panel, P19 (23, 27, 31, 37)(41, 47, 51, 55).
Row 3: (P1, K1) 9 (11, 13, 15, 18)(20, 23, 25, 27) times, P1, work Row 3 of Cable Panel, (P1, K1) 9 (11, 13, 15, 18)(20, 23, 25, 27) times, P1.
Row 4: P19 (23, 27, 31, 37)(41, 47, 51, 55), work Row 4 of Cable Panel, P19 (23, 27, 31, 37)(41, 47, 51, 55).

WE in 4-row Moss Stitch and 24-row Cable Panel (beginning on Row 5) as established until front measures 18 (18, 18.5, 19, 19)(19.5, 20, 20, 20)" from CO edge, ending after WS Row 4 of Moss Stitch pattern.

Armhole Shaping

Keeping in pattern as established, BO 7 (7, 9, 9, 11)(11, 13, 13, 15) sts at beginning of next two rows. 82 (90, 94, 102, 110)(118, 126, 134, 138) sts.

WE until armholes measure 4.5 (5.5, 6.5, 6.5, 7)(7.5, 7.5, 8, 8.25)", ending after a RS row.

Neck Shaping

Next Row (WS): Work as established for 52 (57, 59, 64, 68)(73, 77, 81, 83) sts, Sl last 22 (24, 24, 26, 26)(28, 28, 28, 28) sts just worked onto a st holder or scrap yarn for center neck; work to end.
Cont in pattern on last 30 (33, 35, 38, 42)(45, 49, 53, 55) sts only for left front neck.

Left Front Neck

Dec Row (RS): Work as established to last 2 sts, K2tog. 1 st dec.
Dec Row (WS): P2tog, work to end. 1 st dec.
Rep Dec Rows as established on next 3 (3, 5, 5, 5)(5, 5, 7, 7) rows. 25 (28, 28, 31, 35)(38, 42, 44, 46) sts.
Cont as established and rep RS Dec Row every other row five times. 20 (23, 23, 26, 30)(33, 37, 39, 41) sts.

WE until armhole measures 8 (9, 10, 10.5, 11)(11.5, 12, 12.5, 13)", ending after a WS row.

Left Shoulder

Row 1 (RS): BO 9 (10, 11, 12, 14)(16, 18, 19, 20) sts, work to end.
Row 2 (WS): P across.
BO remaining 11 (13, 12, 14, 16)(17, 19, 20, 21) sts.

Right Front Neck

With RS facing, rejoin yarn to remaining 30 (33, 35, 38, 42)(45, 49, 53, 55) sts for right front neck.
Dec Row (RS): SSK, work to end. 1 st dec.
Dec Row (WS): P to last 2 sts, P2tog TBL. 1 st dec.
Rep Dec Rows as established on next 3 (3, 5, 5, 5)(5, 5, 7, 7) rows. 25 (28, 28, 31, 35)(38, 42, 44, 46) sts.
Cont as established and rep RS Dec Row every other row five times. 20 (23, 23, 26, 30)(33, 37, 39, 41) sts.

WE until armhole measures 8 (9, 10, 10.5, 11)(11.5, 12, 12.5, 13)", or same as left front armhole to shoulders, ending after a RS row.

Right Shoulder

Row 1 (WS): BO 9 (10, 11, 12, 14)(16, 18, 19, 20) sts, P to end.
Row 2 (RS): Work to end.
BO remaining 11 (13, 12, 14, 16)(17, 19, 20, 21) sts.

Back

CO 82 (90, 98, 106, 118)(126, 138, 146, 154) sts.
Row 1 (RS): (K2, P2) to last 2 sts, K2.
Row 2 (WS): (P2, K2) to last 2 sts, P2.
Cont in Rib as established for 3", ending after Row 2.

Next Row (RS): K across.
Beginning with a K row, work five rows in Rev St st.
Next Row (RS): K across.
Next Row (WS): P to last st, M1P, P1. 83 (91, 99, 107, 119)(127, 139, 147, 155) sts.

Body

Work Moss Stitch from chart or written instructions, until back measures same as front from CO edge to armholes, ending after Row 4 of pattern.

Armholes Shaping

Keeping in pattern as established, BO 7 (7, 9, 9, 11)(11, 13, 13, 15) sts at beginning of next two rows. 69 (77, 81, 89, 97)(105, 113, 121, 125) sts.

WE until armholes measure 8 (9, 10, 10.5, 11)(11.5, 12, 12.5, 13)", or same as front armhole to shoulders, ending after a WS row.

Shoulder Shaping

BO 9 (10, 11, 12, 14)(16, 18, 19, 20) sts at beginning of next two rows. 51 (57, 59, 65, 69)(73, 77, 83, 85) sts.
BO 9 (11, 11, 13, 15)(16, 18, 20, 21) sts at beginning of next two rows.
Sl remaining 33 (35, 37, 39, 39)(41, 41, 43, 43) sts onto a st holder or scrap yarn for back neck. Break yarn.

Sleeves (make two the same)

CO 42 (42, 46, 46, 50)(50, 54, 58, 58) sts.
Row 1 (RS): (K2, P2) to last 2 sts, K2.
Row 2: (P2, K2) to last 2 sts, P2.
Cont in Rib as established for 3", ending after Row 2.

Next Row (RS): K across.
Beginning with a K row, work five rows in Rev St st.
Next Row (RS): K across.

Sizes 36 (-, 43, -, 52)(-, -, 64.5, -)" Only
Dec Row (WS): P to last 2 sts, P2tog. 41 (-, 45, -, 49)(-, -, 57, -) sts.

Sizes - (39.5, -, 46.75, -)(55.5, 61, -, 68)" Only
Inc Row (WS): P to last st, M1 P-wise, P1. - (43, -, 47, -)(51, 55, -, 59) sts.

Moss Stitch Section (resume all sizes)

Stitch pattern and increase rows are worked at the same time. Read through instructions before beginning.

Work Rows 1–4 of Moss Stitch from chart or written instructions. Beginning again on Row 1 and working inc sts into pattern as established, work as follows.

Inc Row: K1, M1, work as established to last st, M1, K1. 2 sts inc.
Rep Inc Row every following four rows 5 (10, 22, 23, 24)(25, 26, 27, 28) more times. 53 (65, 91, 95, 99)(103, 109, 113, 117) sts.

Sizes 36 (39.5, -, -, -)(-, -, -, -)" Only
Rep Inc Row every six rows 10 (8, -, -, -)(-, -, -, -) times. 73 (81, -, -, -)(-, -, -, -) sts.

Resume All Sizes
WE until sleeve measures 17 (18, 18, 19, 19)(20, 20, 21, 21)", ending after a WS row.

Sleeve Cap
Mark both ends of last row worked with a removeable st marker or scrap yarn.
WE for 12 (12, 16, 16, 20)(20, 22, 22, 26) rows.
BO loosely in pattern.

Neckband
Join right shoulder seam.
Starting at left shoulder seam, PU and K 17 (17, 18, 20, 20)(20, 22, 23, 23) sts down left front neck, K22 (24, 24, 26, 26)(28, 28, 28, 28) from front neck st holder, PU and K 18 (18, 19, 21, 21)(21, 23, 24, 24) sts up right front neck, K33 (35, 37, 39, 39)(41, 41, 43, 43) from back neck st holder. 90 (94, 98, 106, 106)(110, 114, 118, 118) sts.

Beginning with a K row (WS row), work five rows in Rev St st.
Next Row (RS): K across.
Beginning with Row 2 as given for front, back, and sleeves, work 2x2 Rib for 4".
BO loosely in 2x2 Rib.

Finishing
Join left shoulder and neckband seam.
Fold neckband in half onto WS and slip stitch BO row to picked up edge.
Join side seams and sleeve seams to markers.
Set in sleeves, matching BO sts at underarm to sleeve cap from markers.
Weave in ends, wash, and block to diagram.

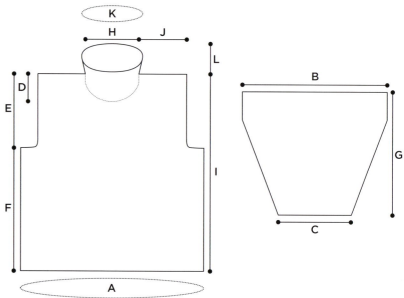

- **A** *chest circumference* 37 (40.5, 44, 47.5, 53)(56.5, 61.5, 65, 69)"
- **B** *upper arm* 16.25 (18, 20.25, 21, 22)(23, 24.25, 25, 26)"
- **C** *wrist* 9 (9.5, 10, 10.5, 10.75)(11.25, 12.25, 12.5, 13)"
- **D** *front neck drop* 3.5 (3.5, 3.5, 4, 4)(4, 4.5, 4.5, 4.75)"
- **E** *armhole length* 8 (9, 10, 10.5, 11)(11.5, 12, 12.5, 13)"
- **F** *side seam* 18 (18, 18.5, 19, 19)(19.5, 20, 20, 20)"
- **G** *sleeve length* 17 (18, 18, 19, 19)(20, 20, 21, 21)"
- **H** *back neck width* 7.25 (7.75, 8.25, 8.75, 8.75)(9, 9, 9.5, 9.5)"
- **I** *length from shoulder* 26 (27, 28.5, 29.5, 30)(31, 32, 32.5, 33)"
- **J** *single shoulder width* 4 (4.75, 5, 5.5, 6.5)(7, 8, 8.75, 9)"
- **K** *neckband circumference around middle, before folding* 18 (18.75, 19.5, 21.25, 21.25)(22, 22.75, 23.5, 23.5)"
- **L** *neckband height (before folding)* 5"

LEGEND

Cable Panel

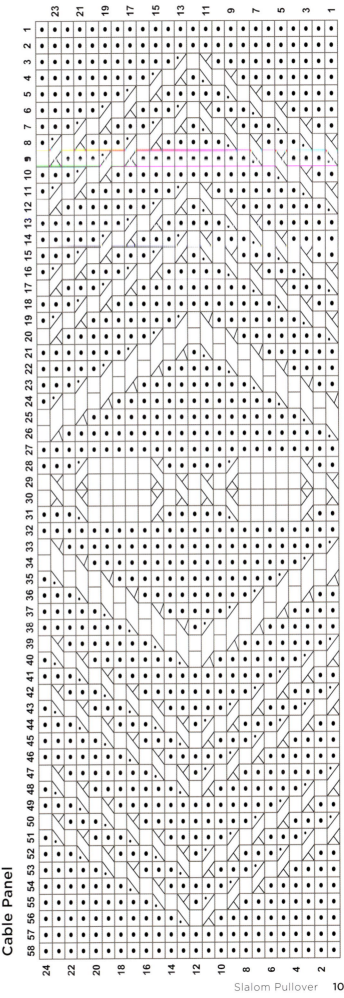

Slalom Pullover

DEILEN HOOD
by Christie Wareham-Norfolk

FINISHED MEASUREMENTS
Cowl: 29" circumference × 11" height
Hood: 23" circumference × 12" height

YARN
Wool of the Andes™ Tweed (worsted weight, 80% Peruvian Highland Wool, 20% Donegal Tweed; 110 yards/50g): MC Prussian Heather 25453, 5 skeins; CC Down Heather 25458, 1 skein (optional, for i-cord tie)

NEEDLES
US 7 (4.5mm) 24–32" circular needles, or size to obtain gauge
US 7 (4.5mm) DPN or straight or circular needle for 3-Needle Bind Off, or size to obtain gauge
US 8 (5mm) 24–32" circular needles, or one size larger than size used to obtain gauge
US 6 (4mm) DPNs or circular needles for I-cord, or one size smaller than size used to obtain gauge

NOTIONS
Yarn Needle
Stitch Markers
Locking Stitch Markers
Cable Needle
Safety Pins

GAUGE
22 sts and 27 rnds = 4" in Cowl Chart pattern, blocked (gauge is not crucial, but it will affect finished size and yardage requirements)
25 sts and 24 rnds = 4" in Cowl Rib in the round, blocked (note that this is approximate due to the amount of stretch in the ribbing)

For pattern support, contact christiewn@westnet.com.au

Deilen Hood

Notes:
The bold cable design on this stylish yet practical hooded cowl picks up the shape of leaves and entwining branches. The cables are simple on the cowl portion and then become more intricate on the sides and back of the hood.

The cowl is knitted in the round, while the hood is worked flat. On finishing the main body of the cowl/hood, stitches are picked up around the front hood opening and a small section at the front of the cowl. A casing is knitted and stitched to the inside of the hood/cowl for an I-cord to be threaded through as the tie.

Charts are worked both in the round and flat. When working charts in the round, read each chart row from right to left as a RS row; when working charts flat, read RS rows (odd numbers) from right to left, and WS rows (even numbers) from left to right.

MC is used throughout. The CC is optional, for the I-Cord Tie.

DIRECTIONS

Cowl
CO 176 sts. Join to work in the rnd, being careful not to twist sts; PM for BOR.

Cowl Rib
Rnd 1: *K2, P1, (K2, P2) two times; rep from * to end.
Rep Rnd 1 nine more times.

Cowl Chart
Rnd 1: Work Rnd 1 of Cowl Chart, repeating section between red lines six times in total. At end of rnd remove BOR M. Sl first 2 sts from LH needle onto RH needle. Replace BOR M.
Rnds 2–23: Work chart rows to end of Rnd 23. Remove BOR M, return last 2 sts worked to LH needle. Replace BOR M. Sl first 2 sts back onto RH needle, counting them as the first 2 worked sts of Rnd 24.
Rnds 24–30: Work to end of Rnd 30. Remove BOR M. Sl first 2 sts from LH needle onto RH needle. Replace BOR M.
Rnds 31–51: Work to end of Rnd 51. Remove BOR M, return last 2 sts worked to LH needle. Replace BOR M. Sl first 2 sts back onto RH needle, counting them as the first 2 worked sts of Rnd 52.
Rnds 52–53: Work as charted.
Rnd 54: Work as charted, working to 7 sts before BOR; BO 19 sts in pattern as established, removing BOR M and placing locking st markers on edges of eighth (marker A, M-A) and tenth (marker B, M-B) bound off sts, which are either side of the central cable st.
Sl last remaining st after BO from RH needle back to LH needle. 157 sts.

Hood
Hood is worked flat.
Rows 1–46: Work Rows 1–46 of Lower Hood Chart, repeating section between red lines five times total. 157 sts.

Work Hood Upper charts consecutively (Right and Left sections form one chart). 96 sts.

Divide sts evenly between two needles. With RS tog, BO using 3-Needle Bind Off.

Casing
With RS of cowl facing and using gauge size needle, PU and K 1 st at M-B, PU and K 9 sts to start of hood, PU and K 2 sts in corner then PU and K every slipped st (86 sts) around hood opening, PU and K 2 sts in corner before cowl then PU and K 8 sts up to and including M-A st. 108 sts.

Row 1 (WS): K across.
Change to larger needles.
Row 2 (RS): K across.
Row 3: P across.
Rep Rows 2–3 two more times.

Break yarn, leaving a tail two times the length of the live sts. Thread yarn through yarn needle then take back through all live sts, dropping sts off knitting needle as you go. Spread sts along tail yarn so they are evenly spaced. Turn casing to inside of hood along outside line of purl sts so it lies flat on the inside. Use safety pins to pin casing to inside of hood at center back and each end onto cowl. Pin at intervals around inside of hood and cowl.
Use yarn tail to stitch casing down along long edge inside hood and cowl. Ensure casing lies flat and take yarn through each edge st on casing and then through one leg of a st of hood/cowl. Leave ends of casing open at center front.

I-Cord Tie
Using CC (if desired) and smaller needles, CO 4 sts and work as I-cord for 47".

Finishing
Weave in ends, wash, and block to diagram.
Attach safety pin to end of tie and thread tie through casing. Remove safety pin.

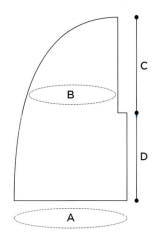

- **A** *cowl circumference* 29"
- **B** *hood circumference* 23"
- **C** *hood height* 12"
- **D** *cowl height* 11"

LEGEND

No Stitch
Placeholder—no stitch made

K
RS: Knit stitch
WS: Purl stitch

P
RS: Purl stitch
WS: Knit stitch

K TBL
RS: Knit stitch through the back loop
WS: Purl stitch through the back loop

Sl
RS: Slip stitch purl-wise, with yarn in back
WS: Slip stitch purl-wise, with yarn in front

K2tog
Knit 2 stitches together as one stitch

SSK
Slip, slip, knit slipped stitches together

K2tog on WS
WS: Knit 2 stitches together as one stitch

BO
Bind off 1 stitch

Pattern Repeat

2 over 2 Right Cable (2/2 RC)
Sl2 to CN, hold in back; K2, K2 from CN

2 over 2 Left Cable (2/2 LC)
Sl2 to CN, hold in front; K2, K2 from CN

2 over 2 Right Cable, Purl back (2/2 RPC)
Sl2 to CN, hold in back; K2, P2 from CN

2 over 2 Left Cable, Purl back (2/2 LPC)
Sl2 to CN, hold in front; P2, K2 from CN

2 over 3 Right Cable (2/3 RC)
Sl3 to CN, hold in back; K2, K3 from CN

2 over 3 Left Cable (2/3 LC)
Sl2 to CN, hold in front; K3, K2 from CN

2 over 2 Right Cable, through back loops (2/2 RC-TBL)
Sl2 to CN, hold in back; K2 TBL, K2 TBL from CN

2 over 2 Left Cable, through back loops (2/2 LC-TBL)
Sl2 to CN, hold in front; K2 TBL, K2 TBL from CN

2 over 3 Left Cable, through back loops (2/3 LC-TBL)
Sl2 to CN, hold in front; K3 TBL, K2 TBL from CN

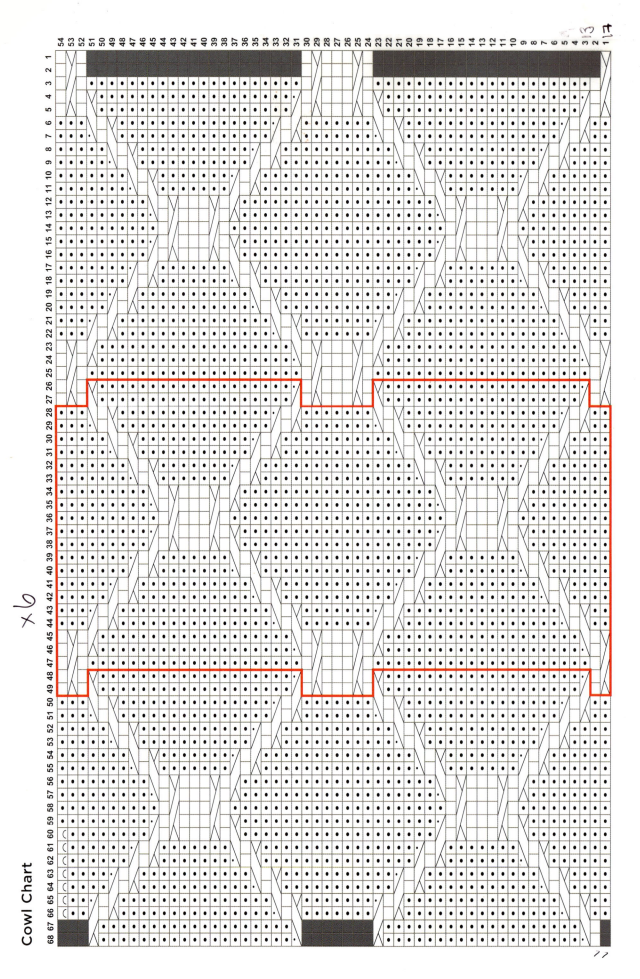

Cowl Chart

110 Deilen Hood

Lower Hood Chart

Hood—Upper Left

Hood—Upper Right

Deilen Hood

KINRIVER
by Amy Snell

FINISHED MEASUREMENTS
63" width × 23.5" length

YARN
Swish™ (bulky weight, 100% Fine Superwash Merino; 137 yards/100g): Garnet Heather 27731, 14 hanks

NEEDLES
US 10 (6mm) 40" circular needles, or size to obtain gauge
US 9 (5.5mm) 16" circular needles, or size to obtain 1x1 Rib gauge

NOTIONS
Yarn Needle
Cable Needle
Scrap Yarn or Spare Circular Needle Cable to hold large number of stitches
Buttons, 1" in diameter (10)
Sewing Needle and Thread
Blocking Pins and/or Wires

GAUGE
12 sts and 20 rows = 4" in Stockinette Stitch, blocked
12 sts and 22 rows = 4" in Seed Stitch, blocked
15 sts and 24 rows = 4" in Garter Stitch, blocked
19 sts and 22 rows = 4" in Diamond Cable and Center Twist Cable Patterns, blocked
24 sts and 24 rnds = 4" in 1x1 Rib in the round on smaller needles, blocked

For pattern support, contact deviousknitter@gmail.com

Kinriver

Notes:

Intricate cables-within-cables wend their way from side to side across the spirited Kinriver poncho, calling to mind meandering rivulets and streams making their way through a lush green countryside. Knit from cozy, soft 100% Merino wool, Kinriver is a flexible layering piece that can be worn open and loose as a traditional poncho, or closed along the bottom edge with buttons that form oversized sleeves.

Kinriver is knit in one piece from side to side, dividing briefly for the neck opening. The 82-stitch cable-and-seed panel is reversed on the back. Two-row buttonholes in the garter-stitch border are worked along with the body, while a cozy ribbed collar is picked up and knit on afterwards.

Charts are worked flat; read RS rows (odd numbers) from right to left, and WS rows (even numbers) from left to right.

The charts which show the patterning on the front and back of the garment are worked six times in total; the second and third repeat of the charts have slight alterations to allow for the neck opening and leave out buttonholes in the center section.

Kinriver's button placement as directed in the pattern leaves a 20" wide center opening, which will accommodate up to 40" waist. If you wish for a wider opening, omitting the fifth and sixth buttonholes will allow for a 30" opening (up to 60" waist); omitting the fourth, fifth, sixth, and seventh buttonholes will allow for a 40" opening (up to 80" waist).

2/2 LC (2 over 2 Left Cable)
Sl2 to CN, hold in front; K2, K2 from CN.

2/2 RC (2 over 2 Right Cable)
Sl2 to CN, hold in back; K2, K2 from CN.

2/2 LPC (2 over 2 Left Cable, Purl back)
Sl2 to CN, hold in front; P2, K2 from CN.

2/2 RPC (2 over 2 Right Cable, Purl back)
Sl2 to CN, hold in back; K2, P2 from CN.

3/3 LC (3 over 3 Left Cable)
Sl3 to CN, hold in front; K3, K3 from CN.

3/3 RC (3 over 3 Right Cable)
Sl3 to CN, hold in back; K3, K3 from CN.

Seed Stitch (flat over a multiple of 2 sts)
Row 1 (RS): (P1, K1) to end.
Row 2 (WS): (K1, P1) to end.
Rep Rows 1–2 for pattern.

Two-Row Buttonhole
Row 1: K1, Sl1, BO the next 2 sts, resume working in pattern.
Row 2: At BO sts, CO 3 sts using Knitted Cast On. Sl third st back to LH needle, K2tog, K1.

Tubular Bind Off
A photo tutorial can be found at knitpicks.com/learning-center/tubular-bind-off.

Front Chart (flat over 82 sts)

Row 1 (RS): K1, Sl1, BO 2 sts, K3, P1, K1, P1, K2, P2, K6, P2, K2, P1, K1, P1, K2, P8, K4, P8, K2, P1, K1, P1, K2, P2, K6, P2, K2, (P1, K1) seven times.

Row 2 (WS): (K1, P1) six times, K1, P3, K2, P6, K2, P3, K1, P3, K8, P4, K8, P3, K1, P3, K2, P6, K2, (P3, K1) two times, CO 3 sts, Sl last st back to LH needle, K2tog, K1.

Row 3: K7, P1, K1, P1, K2, P2, 3/3 LC, P2, K2, P1, K1, P1, K2, P8, 2/2 RC, P8, K2, P1, K1, P1, K2, P2, 3/3 RC, P2, K2, (P1, K1) seven times.

Row 4: (K1, P1) six times, K1, P3, K2, P6, K2, P3, K1, P3, K8, P4, K8, P3, K1, P3, K2, P6, K2, P3, K1, P3, K5.

Row 5: K7, P1, K1, P1, K2, P2, K6, P2, K2, P1, K1, P1, K2, P6, 2/2 RC, 2/2 LC, P6, K2, P1, K1, P1, K2, P2, K6, P2, K2, (P1, K1) seven times.

Row 6: (K1, P1) six times, K1, P3, K2, P6, K2, P3, K1, P3, K6, P8, K6, P3, K1, P3, K2, P6, K2, P3, K1, P3, K5.

Row 7: K7, P1, K1, P1, K2, P2, K1, 2/2 LC, K1, P2, K2, P1, K1, P1, K2, P4, (2/2 RC) two times, 2/2 LC, P4, K2, P1, K1, P1, K2, P2, K1, 2/2 RC, K1, P2, K2, (P1, K1) seven times.

Row 8: (K1, P1) six times, K1, P3, K2, P6, K2, P3, K1, P3, K4, P12, K4, P3, K1, P3, K2, P6, K2, P3, K1, P3, K5.

Row 9: K7, P1, K1, P1, K2, P2, K6, P2, K2, P1, K1, P1, K2, P2, (2/2 RC) two times, (2/2 LC) two times, P2, K2, P1, K1, P1, K2, P2, K6, P2, K2, (P1, K1) seven times.

Row 10: (K1, P1) six times, K1, P3, K2, P6, K2, P3, K1, P3, K2, P16, K2, P3, K1, P3, K2, P6, K2, P3, K1, P3, K5.

Row 11: K7, P1, K1, P1, K2, P2, 3/3 LC, P2, K2, P1, K1, P1, K2, P2, K2, 2/2 RPC, K4, 2/2 LPC, K2, P2, K2, P1, K1, P1, K2, P2, 3/3 RC, P2, K2, (P1, K1) seven times.

Row 12: (K1, P1) six times, K1, P3, K2, P6, K2, P3, K1, P3, (K2, P4) three times, K2, P3, K1, P3, K2, P6, K2, P3, K1, P3, K5.

Row 13: K7, P1, K1, P1, K2, P2, K6, P2, K2, P1, K1, P1, K2, (P2, 2/2 LC) three times, P2, K2, P1, K1, P1, K2, P2, K6, P2, K2, (P1, K1) seven times.

Row 14: Rep Row 12.

Row 15: K7, P1, K1, P1, K2, P2, K1, 2/2 LC, K1, P2, K2, P1, K1, P1, K2, (P2, K4) three times, P2, K2, P1, K1, P1, K2, P2, K1, 2/2 RC, K1, P2, K2, (P1, K1) seven times.

Rows 16–18: Rep Rows 12–14.

Row 19: K7, P1, K1, P1, K2, P2, 3/3 LC, P2, K2, P1, K1, P1, K2, P2, K2, 2/2 LC, K4, 2/2 RC, K2, P2, K2, P1, K1, P1, K2, P2, 3/3 RC, P2, K2, (P1, K1) seven times.

Row 20: Rep Row 10.

Row 21: K7, P1, K1, P1, K2, P2, K6, P2, K2, P1, K1, P1, K2, P2, (2/2 LC) two times, (2/2 RC) two times, P2, K2, P1, K1, P1, K2, P2, K6, P2, K2, (P1, K1) seven times.

Row 22: Rep Row 8.

Row 23: K7, P1, K1, P1, K2, P2, K1, 2/2 LC, K1, P2, K2, P1, K1, P1, K2, P4, 2/2 LC, (2/2 RC) two times, P4, K2, P1, K1, P1, K2, P2, K1, 2/2 RC, K1, P2, K2, (P1, K1) seven times.

Row 24: Rep Row 6.

Row 25: K7, P1, K1, P1, K2, P2, K6, P2, K2, P1, K1, P1, K2, P6, 2/2 LC, 2/2 RC, P6, K2, P1, K1, P1, K2, P2, K6, P2, K2, (P1, K1) seven times.
Row 26: Rep Row 4.
Rows 27-28: Rep Rows 3-4.
Row 29-30: Rep Rows 1-2.
Row 31: K7, P1, K1, P1, K2, P2, K1, 2/2 LC, K1, P2, K2, P1, K1, P1, K2, P8, 2/2 RC, P8, K2, P1, K1, P1, K2, P2, K1, 2/2 RC, K1, P2, K2, (P1, K1) seven times.
Rows 32-34: Rep Rows 4-6.
Row 35: K7, P1, K1, P1, K2, P2, 3/3 LC, P2, K2, P1, K1, P1, K2, P4, (2/2 RC) two times, 2/2 LC, P4, K2, P1, K1, P1, K2, P2, 3/3 RC, P2, K2, (P1, K1) seven times.
Rows 36-38: Rep Rows 8-10.
Row 39: K7, P1, K1, P1, K2, P2, K1, 2/2 LC, K1, P2, K2, P1, K1, P1, K2, P2, K2, 2/2 RPC, K4, 2/2 LPC, K2, P2, K2, P1, K1, P1, K2, P2, K1, 2/2 RC, K1, P2, K2, (P1, K1) seven times.
Row 40-42: Rep Rows 12-14.
Row 43: K7, P1, K1, P1, K2, P2, 3/3 LC, P2, K2, P1, K1, P1, K2, (P2, K4) three times, P2, K2, P1, K1, P1, K2, P2, 3/3 RC, P2, K2, (P1, K1) seven times.
Row 44-46: Rep Rows 12-14.
Row 47: K7, P1, K1, P1, K2, P2, K1, 2/2 LC, K1, P2, K2, P1, K1, P1, K2, P2, K2, 2/2 LC, K4, 2/2 RC, K2, P2, K2, P1, K1, P1, K2, P2, K1, 2/2 RC, K1, P2, K2, (P1, K1) seven times.
Row 48: Rep Row 10.
Row 49: Rep Row 21.
Row 50: Rep Row 8.
Row 51: K7, P1, K1, P1, K2, P2, 3/3 LC, P2, K2, P1, K1, P1, K2, P4, 2/2 LC, 2/2 RC two times, P4, K2, P1, K1, P1, K2, P2, 3/3 RC, P2, K2, (P1, K1) seven times.
Row 52: Rep Row 6.
Row 53: Rep Row 25.
Row 54: Rep Row 4.
Row 55: Rep Row 31.
Row 56: Rep Row 4.
Rep Rows 1-56 for pattern.

Back Chart (flat over 82 sts)

Row 1 (RS): (P1, K1) six times, P1, K3, P2, K6, P2, K2, P1, K1, P1, K2, P8, K4, P8, K2, P1, K1, P1, K2, P2, K6, P2, K2, P1, K1, P1, K7.
Row 2 (WS): K5, P3, K1, P3, K2, P6, K2, P3, K1, P3, K8, P4, K8, P3, K1, P3, K2, P6, K2, P2, (K1, P1) seven times.
Row 3: (P1, K1) six times, P1, K3, P2, 3/3 LC, P2, K2, P1, K1, P1, K2, P8, 2/2 LC, P8, K2, P1, K1, P1, K2, P2, 3/3 RC, P2, K2, P1, K1, P1, K7.
Row 4: Rep Row 2.
Row 5: (P1, K1) six times, P1, K3, P2, K6, P2, K2, P1, K1, P1, K2, P6, 2/2 RC, 2/2 LC, P6, K2, P1, K1, P1, K2, P2, K6, P2, K2, P1, K1, P1, K7.
Row 6: K5, P3, K1, P3, K2, P6, K2, P3, K1, P3, K6, P8, K6, P3, K1, P3, K2, P6, K2, P2, (K1, P1) seven times.
Row 7: (P1, K1) six times, P1, K3, P2, K1, 2/2 LC, K1, P2, K2, P1, K1, P1, K2, P4, 2/2 RC, (2/2 LC) two times, P4, K2, P1, K1, P1, K2, P2, K1, 2/2 RC, K1, P2, K2, P1, K1, P1, K7.
Row 8: K5, P3, K1, P3, K2, P6, K2, P3, K1, P3, K4, P12, K4, P3, K1, P3, K2, P6, K2, P2, (K1, P1) seven times.
Row 9: (P1, K1) six times, P1, K3, P2, K6, P2, K2, P1, K1, P1, K2, P2, (2/2 RC) two times, (2/2 LC) two times, P2, K2, P1, K1, P1, K2, P2, K6, P2, K2, P1, K1, P1, K7.
Row 10: K5, P3, K1, P3, K2, P6, K2, P3, K1, P3, K2, P16, K2, P3, K1, P3, K2, P6, K2, P2, (K1, P1) seven times.
Row 11: (P1, K1) six times, P1, K3, P2, 3/3 LC, P2, K2, P1, K1, P1, K2, P2, K2, 2/2 RPC, K4, 2/2 LPC, K2, P2, K2, P1, K1, P1, K2, P2, 3/3 RC, P2, K2, P1, K1, P1, K7.
Row 12: K5, P3, K1, P3, K2, P6, K2, P3, K1, P3, (K2, P4) three times, K2, P3, K1, P3, K2, P6, K2, P2, (K1, P1) seven times.
Row 13: (P1, K1) six times, P1, K3, P2, K6, P2, K2, P1, K1, P1, K2, (P2, 2/2 RC) three times, P2, K2, P1, K1, P1, K2, P2, K6, P2, K2, P1, K1, P1, K7.
Row 14: Rep Row 12.
Row 15: (P1, K1) six times, P1, K3, P2, K1, 2/2 LC, K1, P2, K2, P1, K1, P1, K2, (P2, K4) three times, P2, K2, P1, K1, P1, K2, P2, K1, 2/2 RC, K1, P2, K2, P1, K1, P1, K7.
Rows 16-18: Rep Rows 12-14.
Row 19: (P1, K1) six times, P1, K3, P2, 3/3 LC, P2, K2, P1, K1, P1, K2, P2, K2, 2/2 LC, K4, 2/2 RC, K2, P2, K2, P1, K1, P1, K2, P2, 3/3 RC, P2, K2, P1, K1, P1, K7.
Row 20: Rep Row 10.
Row 21: (P1, K1) six times, P1, K3, P2, K6, P2, K2, P1, K1, P1, K2, P2, (2/2 LC) two times, (2/2 RC) two times, P2, K2, P1, K1, P1, K2, P2, K6, P2, K2, P1, K1, P1, K7.
Row 22: Rep Row 8.
Row 23: (P1, K1) six times, P1, K3, P2, K1, 2/2 LC, K1, P2, K2, P1, K1, P1, K2, P4, (2/2 LC) two times, 2/2 RC, P4, K2, P1, K1, P1, K2, P2, K1, 2/2 RC, K1, P2, K2, P1, K1, P1, K7.
Row 24: Rep Row 6.
Row 25: (P1, K1) six times, P1, K3, P2, K6, P2, K2, P1, K1, P1, K2, P6, 2/2 LC, 2/2 RC, P6, K2, P1, K1, P1, K2, P2, K6, P2, K2, P1, K1, P1, K7.
Row 26-27: Rep Rows 2-3.
Row 28: Rep Row 2.
Row 29-30: Rep Rows 1-2.
Row 31: (P1, K1) six times, P1, K3, P2, K1, 2/2 LC, K1, P2, K2, P1, K1, P1, K2, P8, 2/2 LC, P8, K2, P1, K1, P1, K2, P2, K1, 2/2 RC, K1, P2, K2, P1, K1, P1, K7.
Row 32-34: Rep Rows 4-6.
Row 35: (P1, K1) six times, P1, K3, P2, 3/3 LC, P2, K2, P1, K1, P1, K2, P4, 2/2 RC, (2/2 LC) two times, P4, K2, P1, K1, P1, K2, P2, 3/3 RC, P2, K2, P1, K1, P1, K7.
Row 36-38: Rep Rows 8-10.
Row 39: (P1, K1) six times, P1, K3, P2, K1, 2/2 LC, K1, P2, K2, P1, K1, P1, K2, P2, K2, 2/2 RPC, K4, 2/2 LPC, K2, P2, K2, P1, K1, P1, K2, P2, K1, 2/2 RC, K1, P2, K2, P1, K1, P1, K7.
Row 40-42: Rep Rows 12-14.
Row 43: (P1, K1) six times, P1, K3, P2, 3/3 LC, P2, K2, P1, K1, P1, K2, (P2, K4) three times, P2, K2, P1, K1, P1, K2, P2, 3/3 RC, P2, K2, P1, K1, P1, K7.
Row 44-46: Rep Rows 12-14.
Row 47: (P1, K1) six times, P1, K3, P2, K1, 2/2 LC, K1, P2, K2, P1, K1, P1, K2, P2, K2, 2/2 LC, K4, 2/2 RC, K2, P2, K2, P1, K1, P1, K2, P2, K1, 2/2 RC, K1, P2, K2, P1, K1, P1, K7.
Row 48: Rep Row 10.
Row 49: Rep Row 21.

Row 50: Rep Row 8.
Row 51: (P1, K1) six times, P1, K3, P2, 3/3 LC, P2, K2, P1, K1, P1, K2, P4, (2/2 LC) two times, 2/2 RC, P4, K2, P1, K1, P1, K2, P2, 3/3 RC, P2, K2, P1, K1, P1, K7.
Row 52: Rep Row 6.
Row 53: (P1, K1) six times, P1, K3, P2, K6, P2, K2, P1, K1, P1, K2, P6, 2/2 LC, 2/2 RC, P2, K1, P3, K2, P1, K1, P1, K2, P2, K6, P2, K2, P1, K1, P1, K7.
Row 54: Rep Row 2.
Row 55: Rep Row 31.
Row 56: Rep Row 2.
Rep Rows 1–56 for pattern.

DIRECTIONS

Body
Loosely CO 164 sts.
Work Seed Stitch for four rows.

Next Row (RS): Work Front Chart then Back Chart, from charts or written instructions.
Next Row (WS): Work next row of Back Chart then Front Chart.
Cont as established, working through the complete charts twice.
Work Rows 1–28 of charts one more time. Two and a half chart reps have been worked in total to this point.

Divide for Neck
Place 82 sts for front onto scrap yarn or spare cable.

Back Center
Working across the 82 back sts only, join a new ball of yarn ready to begin a RS row.
Work remaining 28 rows of Back Chart (Rows 29–56).
Work Rows 1–28 of Back Chart once more.
Break yarn, leaving tail at least 6″ long for weaving in.
Three and a half chart reps have been worked in total to this point on the back.

Front Neck Decreases
Working across the 82 front sts only, resume with Row 29 of Front Chart, replacing buttonhole (BO and CO) sts in Rows 29 and 30 with K sts, and AT THE SAME TIME work shaping as follows.
Row 1 (RS): K4, work Front Chart Row 29 as established from St 5 to last 2 sts, K2tog. 81 sts.
Row 2 (WS): P2tog, work across remainder of Front Chart Row 30. 80 sts.
Row 3: Work next row of Front Chart to last 2 sts, K2tog. 1 st dec.
Row 4: P2tog, work across remainder of Front Chart. 1 st dec.
Rep Rows 3–4 three more times. 72 sts.

Front Center
Work Rows 39–56 of Front Chart as established, working only st columns 1–72.
Work Rows 1–18 of Front Chart once more, replacing buttonhole sts in Rows 1 and 2 with K sts.

Front Neck Increases
Proceed from Row 19 of Front Chart.
Row 1: Work across next row of Front Chart to last st, KFB. 1 st inc.
Row 2: KFB, work across next row of Front Chart. 1 st inc.
Rep Rows 1-2 four more times, ending on Row 28 of Front Chart. 82 sts.
Three and a half chart reps have been worked in total to this point on the front.

Resume Body
Replace held back sts onto working needle.
Resume working Rows 29-56 of Front Chart and Back Chart as established, replacing buttonhole sts in Rows 29 and 30 of Front Chart with K sts.
Four chart reps have been worked in total to this point.
Work Front and Back Charts as established two more times. Work an extra buttonhole in Rows 55 and 56 of final rep of Front Chart.
Six chart reps have been worked.

Work Seed Stitch for four rnds.
BO loosely.

Blocking
For best results, weave in ends, wash and block to a rectangular shape before knitting on the collar, taking care not to stretch the cables.

Collar
Using smaller needles, PU and K 130 sts evenly around neck opening.
Work 1x1 Rib for 2.5".

BO using the Tubular Bind Off.

Finishing
Weave in remaining ends and lightly block the collar, taking care not to stretch.

- **A** wingspan 63"
- **B** width (double the height of finished poncho) 47"
- **C** neck opening 15"

LEGEND

K
RS: Knit stitch
WS: Purl stitch

P
RS: Purl stitch
WS: Knit stitch

Sl
Slip stitch purl-wise, with yarn in back

2 over 2 Right Cable (2/2 RC)
Sl2 to CN, hold in back; K2, K2 from CN

2 over 2 Left Cable (2/2 LC)
Sl2 to CN, hold in front; K2, K2 from CN

2 over 2 Right Cable, Purl back (2/2 RPC)
Sl2 to CN, hold in back; K2, P2 from CN

2 over 2 Left Cable, Purl back (2/2 LPC)
Sl2 to CN, hold in front; P2, K2 from CN

3 over 3 Right Cable (3/3 RC)
Sl3 to CN, hold in back; K3, K3 from CN

3 over 3 Left Cable (3/3 LC)
Sl3 to CN, hold in front; K3, K3 from CN

CO
Cast on 1 stitch

BO
Bind off 1 stitch

Front Chart

Back Chart

Kinriver

EMRE PULLOVER & CARDIGAN
by Todd Gocken

FINISHED MEASUREMENTS
34 (38, 42, 46, 50)(54, 58, 62, 66)" finished chest circumference; meant to be worn with 2–4" positive ease
Samples are 38" (cardigan) & 42" (pullover); models are 35" except short-haired male model is 38"

YARN
High Desert™ (worsted weight, 100% American Wool; 217 yards/100g): Cottonwood 29263 or Riverbend 29268, 8 (10, 11, 12, 13)(14, 16, 17, 18) skeins

NEEDLES
US 7 (4.5mm) circular needles (24" or longer), or size to obtain gauge
US 7 (4.5mm) DPNs or two circular needles for two circulars technique or 32" or longer circular needles for Magic Loop technique, or size to obtain gauge
US 5 (3.75mm) DPNs or 32" circular needles for Magic Loop technique, or two sizes smaller than size used to obtain gauge
US 5 (3.75mm) circular needles (24" or longer), or two sizes smaller than size used to obtain gauge

NOTIONS
Yarn Needle
Stitch Markers
Cable Needle
Scrap Yarn or Stitch Holder
Blocking Pins and/or Wires
Zipper for Cardigan (length of approx 22 (23, 24.5, 25.5, 26.25)(27.5, 28.5, 29, 29.5)")

GAUGE
20 sts and 28 rows = 4" in Moss Stitch, blocked
20 sts = 3" in Chevron Cable, blocked
10 sts = 1.5" in Braided Cable, blocked
12 sts = 2" in Diamond Chart 1, blocked
14 sts = 2.75" in Diamond Chart 2, blocked
18 sts = 3.25" in Diamond Chart 3, blocked

For pattern support, contact todd@toddgockendesigns.com

Emre Pullover & Cardigan

Notes:
Emre was inspired by a mother who wanted the perfect sweater pattern to knit for her son. His personal taste influenced the overall design, so the pattern was named after him.

Emre utilizes traditional Aran patterning and seamless gansey construction. Both versions are knit bottom up; the pullover is made in the round to the armholes, then the front and back are worked flat. Both versions are connected with saddles at the shoulder, then stitches are picked up around the armholes, and sleeves knit from the top down.

Charts are worked both in the round and flat. When working charts in the round, read each chart row from right to left as a RS row; when working charts flat, read RS rows (even numbers) from right to left, and WS rows (odd numbers) from left to right. Always work the Diamonds Chart for the size being made.

Sometimes stitch pattern segments will end before the end of the pattern repeat. Always make sure stitches align in the stitch pattern as intended. (For example, Moss Stitch may sometimes be worked over a multiple of 4 stitches plus 2. If working flat, if a pattern Row 1 ends with K2, then begin that segment on the following WS row with P2.)

3x3 Rib (in the round over a multiple of 6 sts)
All Rnds: (K3, P3) to end.

Moss Stitch (in the round over a multiple of 4 sts)
Rnds 1-2: (K2, P2) to end.
Rnds 3-4: (P2, K2) to end.
Rep Rnds 1-4 for pattern.

Moss Stitch (flat over a multiple of 4 sts)
Rows 1-2: (K2, P2) to end.
Rows 3-4: (P2, K2) to end.
Rep Rows 1-4 for pattern.

PULLOVER DIRECTIONS

Body
Using smaller needles, CO 204 (216, 252, 276, 300)(324, 348, 372, 396) sts using a Cable Cast On. Join to work in the rnd, being careful not to twist sts. PM for BOR.
Work 3x3 Rib for 2 (2, 2.25, 2.25, 2.5)(2.5, 2.5, 2.5, 2.5)".

Next Rnd: Switch to larger needles, *K41 (43, 252, 276, 300)(65, 70, 74, 79), M1 (1, 0, 0, 0)(1, 1, 1, 1); rep from * 3 (3, 0, 0, 0)(3, 3, 3, 3) more times, K to end. 208 (220, 252, 276, 300)(328, 352, 376, 400) sts.

Sizes 34 (38, -, -, -)(-, -, -, -)" Only
*Work Moss Stitch over 16 (18, -, -, -)(-, -, -, -) sts, P2, work Diamonds Chart, work Braided Cable Chart, work Chevron Chart over 40 sts, work Braided Cable Chart, work Diamonds Chart, P2; rep from * once more.

Sizes - (-, 42, 46, 50)(54, 58, 62, 66)" Only
*Work Moss Stitch over - (-, 18, 22, 22)(28, 28, 32, 32) sts, work Braided Cable Chart, work Diamonds Chart, work Braided Cable Chart, work Chevron Chart over - (-, 40, 40, 60)(60, 80, 80, 100) sts, work Braided Cable Chart, work Diamonds Chart, work Braided Cable Chart; rep from * once more.

Resume All Sizes
WE as established, following the charts, until body measures 17 (18, 19, 19.5, 20)(20.5, 21, 21, 21)" from CO edge, ending before an odd (non-cabling) rnd.

Back
Setup (RS): K1, place the following 14 (16, 16, 20, 20)(26, 26, 30, 30) sts onto scrap yarn or st holder, turn work.

Sizes 34 (38, -, -, -)(-, -, -, -)" Only
Row 1 (WS): Sl1, K2, work Diamonds Chart, work Braided Cable Chart, work Chevron Chart over 40 sts, work Braided Cable Chart, work Diamonds Chart, K2, P1, turn work.
Row 2 (RS): Sl1, P2, work Diamonds Chart, work Braided Cable Chart, work Chevron Chart over 40 sts, work Braided Cable Chart, work Diamonds Chart, P2, K1.
Rep Rows 1–2 another 30 (31, -, -, -)(-, -, -, -) times.

Sizes - (-, 42, 46, 50)(54, 58, 62, 66)" Only
Row 1 (WS): Sl1, work Braided Cable Chart, work Diamonds Chart, work Braided Cable Chart, work Chevron Chart over - (-, 40, 40, 60)(60, 80, 80, 100) sts, work Braided Cable Chart, work Diamonds Chart, work Braided Cable Chart, P1, turn work.
Row 2 (RS): Sl1, work Braided Cable Chart, work Diamonds Chart, work Braided Cable Chart, work Chevron Chart over - (-, 40, 40, 60)(60, 80, 80, 100) sts, work Braided Cable Chart, work Diamonds Chart, work Braided Cable Chart, K1, turn work.
Rep Rows 1–2 another - (-, 33, 34, 36)(37, 39, 40, 42) times.

Resume All Sizes
Work Row 1 (WS) as above once more.
Final Back Row (RS): Sl1, K2tog 17 (18, 21, 22, 24)(25, 27, 28, 30) times, K1, PM, K18 (18, 22, 26, 30)(34, 38, 42, 46), PM, K1, K2tog 17 (18, 21, 22, 24)(25, 27, 28, 30) times, K1. Break yarn.

Front
Join new ball at right front.

Sizes 34 (38, -, -, -)(-, -, -, -)" Only
Row 1 (WS): Sl1, K2, work Diamonds Chart, work Braided Cable Chart, work Chevron Chart over 40 sts, work Braided Cable Chart, work Diamonds Chart, K2, P1, turn work. At end of first row, place the following 14 (16, -, -, -)(-, -, -, -) unworked sts onto scrap yarn or st holder.
Row 2 (RS): Sl1, P2, work Diamonds Chart, work Braided Cable Chart, work Chevron Chart over 40 sts, work Braided Cable Chart, work Diamonds Chart, P2, K1.

Sizes - (-, 42, 46, 50)(54, 58, 62, 66)" Only

Row 1 (WS): Sl1, work Braided Cable Chart, work Diamonds Chart, work Braided Cable Chart, work Chevron Chart over - (-, 40, 40, 60)(60, 80, 80, 100) sts, work Braided Cable Chart, work Diamonds Chart, work Braided Cable Chart, P1, turn work. At end of first row, place the following - (-, 16, 20, 20)(20, 20, 30, 30) unworked sts onto scrap yarn or st holder.
Row 2 (RS): Sl1, work Braided Cable Chart, work Diamonds Chart, work Braided Cable Chart, work Chevron Chart over - (-, 40, 40, 60)(60, 80, 80, 100) sts, work Braided Cable Chart, work Diamonds Chart, work Braided Cable Chart, K1, turn work.

Resume All Sizes

Rep Rows 1-2 as established 18 (19, 21, 22, 24)(25, 27, 28, 30) more times.
On last row (RS), work 39 (41, 47, 49, 53)(55, 59, 61, 65) sts, PM, work 12 (12, 16, 20, 24)(28, 32, 36, 40) center sts, PM, work to end of row.

Neck Shaping

Row 1 (RS): Work as established to first M, turn work.
Row 2 (WS): SSK, work to end, turn work. 1 st dec.
Rep Rows 1-2 two more times, slipping first st on each RS row. 36 (38, 44, 46, 50)(52, 56, 58, 62) sts.
Last Row (RS): Sl1, K2tog 17 (18, 21, 22, 24)(25, 27, 28, 30) times, K1. 19 (20, 23, 24, 26)(27, 29, 30, 32) sts.

Place the 12 (12, 16, 20, 24)(28, 32, 36, 40) sts between Ms onto scrap yarn or st holder.

Join new ball of yarn at left neck M.
Row 1 (RS): Work to end of row as established.
Row 2 (WS): Work as established to last 2 sts, K2tog. 1 st dec.
Rep Rows 1-2 two more times, slipping first st on each row. 36 (38, 44, 46, 50)(52, 56, 58, 62) sts.
Last Row (RS): Sl1, K2tog 17 (18, 21, 22, 24)(25, 27, 28, 30) times, K1. 19 (20, 23, 24, 26)(27, 29, 30, 32) sts.
Break yarn.

Left Saddle Shoulder

Saddle is worked from top at neck down to outside of shoulder. Place left shoulder sts on needle as follows: Starting at front left neck edge, place 19 (20, 23, 24, 26)(27, 29, 30, 32) left shoulder sts onto needle, then starting at shoulder edge, place 19 (20, 23, 24, 26)(27, 29, 30, 32) left back shoulder sts onto needle, ending at M. 38 (40, 46, 48, 52)(54, 58, 60, 64) st on the needles
On larger separate needle or DPN, CO 26 sts using a Provisional Cast On method.
Setup Row (working into Provisional CO sts): P1, PM, K2, work Sleeve Chevron Braided Cable Chart over 20 sts, K2, PM, P1, turn work.
Row 1 (RS): Sl1, SM, P2, work Sleeve Chevron Braided Cable Chart over 20 sts, P2, SM, SSK (working last saddle st tog with a back shoulder st), turn work. 1 st dec.
Row 2 (WS): Sl1, SM, K2, work Sleeve Chevron Braided Cable Chart over 20 sts, K2, SM, P2tog (working last saddle st tog with a front shoulder st), turn work. 1 st dec.
Rep Rows 1-2 until all shoulder sts are used up, ending with a WS row. 26 sts.

Left Sleeve

Setup Rnd (RS): Sl1, SM (this M is BOR M), P2, work Sleeve Chevron Braided Cable Chart as established over 20 sts, P2, SM, K1, PU and K 31 (32, 34, 35, 37)(38, 40, 41, 43) sts from back armhole, work 14 (16, 16, 20, 20)(26, 26, 30, 30) held underarm sts in Moss Stitch, PU and K 19 (20, 22, 23, 25)(26, 28, 29, 31) sts from front armhole, K1, SM. 90 (94, 98, 104, 108)(116, 120, 126, 130) sts.

Rnd 1: P2, work Sleeve Chevron Braided Cable Chart over 20 sts, P2, SM, K1, work Moss Stitch to last st, K1.
Dec Rnd: P2, work Sleeve Chevron Braided Cable Chart over 20 sts, P2, SM, SSK, work Moss Stitch to last 2 sts, K2tog. 2 sts dec.
Cont as established and rep Dec Rnd every six rnds 20 (19, 21, 21, 23)(24, 23, 26, 25) more times. 48 (54, 54, 60, 60)(66, 72, 72, 78) sts.
Cont as established without decs until sleeve measures 20 (20.25, 20.75, 21.25, 21.5)(22, 22.5, 23, 23.5)" from Setup Rnd, or 2 (2, 2.25, 2.25, 2.5)(2.5, 2.5, 2.5, 2.5)" less than desired length.

Switch to smaller needles and work 3x3 Rib for 2 (2, 2.25, 2.25, 2.5)(2.5, 2.5, 2.5, 2.5)".
BO in pattern.

Right Saddle Shoulder

Place right shoulder sts on needle as follows: Starting at front right neck edge, place 19 (20, 23, 24, 26)(27, 29, 30, 32) right shoulder sts onto needle, then continuing at shoulder edge, place 19 (20, 23, 24, 26)(27, 29, 30, 32) right back shoulder sts onto needle, ending at M. 38 (40, 46, 48, 52)(54, 58, 60, 64) st on the needles

On larger separate needle or DPN, CO 26 sts using a Provisional Cast On method. **Setup Row:** P1, PM, K2, work Sleeve Chevron Braided Cable Chart over 20 sts, K2, PM, P1, turn work.
Row 1 (RS): Sl1, SM, P2, work Sleeve Chevron Braided Cable Chart over 20 sts, P2, SM, SSK (working last saddle st tog with a front shoulder st), turn work. 1 st dec.
Row 2 (WS): Sl1, SM, K2, work Sleeve Chevron Braided Cable Chart over 20 sts, K2, SM, P2tog (working last saddle st tog with a back shoulder st), turn work. 1 st dec.
Rep Rows 1-2 until all shoulder sts are used up, ending with a WS row. 26 sts.

Right Sleeve

Setup Rnd (RS): Sl1, SM (this M is BOR M), P2, work Sleeve Chevron Braided Cable Chart over 20 sts, P2, SM, K1, PU and K 19 (20, 22, 23, 25)(26, 28, 29, 31) sts from front armhole, work 14 (16, 16, 20, 20)(26, 26, 30, 30) underarm sts in Moss Stitch, PU and K 31 (32, 34, 35, 37)(38, 40, 41, 43) sts from back armhole, K1, SM. 90 (94, 98, 104, 108)(116, 120, 126, 130) sts.

Rnd 1: P2, work Sleeve Chevron Braided Cable Chart over 20 sts, P2, SM, K1, work Moss Stitch to last st, K1.
Dec Rnd: P2, work Sleeve Chevron Braided Cable Chart for 20 sts, P2, SM, SSK, work Moss st to last 2 sts, K2tog. 2 sts dec.

Cont as established and rep Dec Rnd every six rnds 20 (19, 21, 21, 23)(24, 23, 26, 25) more times. 48 (54, 54, 60, 60)(66, 72, 72, 78) sts remain.

Cont as established without decs until sleeve measures 20 (20.25, 20.75, 21.25, 21.5)(22, 22.5, 23, 23.5)" from Setup Rnd, or 2 (2, 2.25, 2.25, 2.5)(2.5, 2.5, 2.5, 2.5)" less than desired length.

Switch to smaller needles and work 3x3 Rib for 2 (2, 2.25, 2.25, 2.5)(2.5, 2.5, 2.5, 2.5)".
BO in pattern.

Neck

With smaller needles and starting at back right shoulder, K18 (18, 22, 26, 30)(34, 38, 42, 46) sts across back neck, K26 sts from left saddle, PU and K 6 sts from left front, K12 (12, 16, 20, 24)(28, 32, 36, 40) held sts from front, PU and K 6 sts from right front, K26 sts from right saddle. 94 (94, 102, 110, 118)(126, 134, 142, 150) sts.

Setup Rnd: *K31 (31, 102, 22, 39)(126, 27, 47, 150), M1 (1, 0, 1, 1)(0, 1, 1, 0); rep from * 1 (1, 0, 3, 1)(0, 3, 1, 0) more times, K remaining 32(32, 0, 22, 40) (0, 26, 48, 0) sts to end. 96 (96, 102, 114, 120)(126, 138, 144, 150) sts.

Rnd 1: (K3, P3) to end.
Rep Rnd 1 for 1.75".
Next Rnd: P all.
Next Rnd: (P3, K3) to end.
Rep last rnd for 1.75".
BO loosely in pattern. Sew BO edge to inside of collar.

Finishing

Weave in all ends, wash, and block to measurements.

CARDIGAN DIRECTIONS

Body

Using smaller needles, CO 215 (227, 257, 281, 305)(335, 359, 383, 407) sts using a Cable Cast On.

Row 1 (RS): K4, (P3, K3) to the last 7 sts, P3, Sl4.
Row 2 (WS): P4, (K3, P3) to last 7 sts, K3, Sl4.
Rep Rows 1-2 until piece measures 2 (2, 2.25, 2.25, 2.5)(2.5, 2.5, 2.5, 2.5)" from CO edge.

Inc Rnd (RS): Switch to larger needles, *K108 (114, 64, 70, 76)(168, 180, 192, 204), M1; rep from * 0 (0, 2, 2, 2)(0, 0, 0, 0) more times, K to end. 1 (1, 3, 3, 3)(1, 1, 1, 1) sts inc. 216 (228, 260, 284, 308)(336, 360, 384, 408) sts.

Row 1 (WS): P4, work Chevron Chart over 20 (20, 20, 20, 30)(30, 40, 40, 50) sts — for sizes - (-, -, -, 50)(54, -, -, 66)" start Chevron Chart with st 11 — work Braided Cable Chart, work Diamonds Chart, K2 (2, 0, 0, 0)(0, 0, 0, 0), work Braided Cable Chart 0 (0, 1, 1, 1)(1, 1, 1, 1) times, work 16 (18, 18, 22, 22)(28, 28, 32, 32) sts in Moss Stitch, K2 (2, 0, 0, 0)(0, 0, 0, 0), work Braided Cable Chart 0 (0, 1, 1, 1)(1, 1, 1, 1) times, work Diamonds Chart, work Braided Cable Chart, work Chevron Chart over the next 40 (40, 40, 40, 60)(60, 80, 80, 100) sts, work Braided Cable Chart, work Diamonds Chart, K2 (2, 0, 0, 0)(0, 0, 0, 0), work Braided Cable Chart 0 (0, 1, 1, 1)(1, 1, 1, 1) times, work 16 (18, 18, 22, 22)(28, 28, 32, 32) sts in Moss Stitch, K2 (2, 0, 0, 0)(0, 0, 0, 0), work Braided Cable Chart 0 (0, 1, 1, 1)(1, 1, 1, 1) times, work Diamonds Chart, work Braided Cable Chart, work Chevron Chart over 20 (20, 20, 20, 30)(30, 40, 40, 50) sts, Sl4.

Row 2 (RS): K4, work Chevron Chart over 20 (20, 20, 20, 30)(30, 40, 40, 50) sts — for sizes - (-, -, -, 50)(54, -, -, 66)" start Chevron Chart with st 11 — work Braided Cable Chart, work Diamonds Chart, P2 (2, 0, 0, 0)(0, 0, 0, 0), work Braided Cable Chart 0 (0, 1, 1, 1)(1, 1, 1, 1) times, work 16 (18, 18, 22, 22)(28, 28, 32, 32) sts in Moss Stitch, P2 (2, 0, 0, 0)(0, 0, 0, 0), work Braided Cable Chart 0 (0, 1, 1, 1)(1, 1, 1, 1) times, work Diamonds Chart, work Braided Cable Chart, work Chevron Chart over 40 (40, 40, 40, 60)(60, 80, 80, 100) sts, work Braided Cable Chart, work Diamonds Chart, P2 (2, 0, 0, 0)(0, 0, 0, 0), work Braided Cable Chart 0 (0, 1, 1, 1)(1, 1, 1, 1) times, work 16 (18, 18, 22, 22)(28, 28, 32, 32) sts in Moss Stitch, P2 (2, 0, 0, 0)(0, 0, 0, 0), work Braided Cable Chart 0 (0, 1, 1, 1)(1, 1, 1, 1) times, work Diamonds Chart, work Braided Cable Chart, work Chevron Chart over 20 (20, 20, 20, 30)(30, 40, 40, 50) sts, Sl4.

Rep Rows 1-2 until piece measures 17 (18, 19, 19.5, 20)(20.5, 21, 21, 21)" from CO edge, ending after a WS row.

Right Front

Starting on a RS row, work 48 (50, 58, 62, 68)(72, 78, 82, 88) sts as established, K1, place the following 14 (16, 16, 20, 20)(26, 26, 30, 30) sts onto scrap yarn or st holder for underarm, turn work.

Cont working right front sts only as established for 37 (39, 43, 45, 49)(51, 55, 57, 61) more rows, slipping the first st of every WS row. 49 (51, 59, 63, 69)(73, 79, 83, 89) sts.

Neck Shaping
Setup Row (RS): Work 10 (10, 12, 14, 16)(18, 20, 22, 24) sts as established, PM, SSK, work to end, turn work. 38 (40, 46, 48, 52)(54, 58, 60, 64) sts.
Row 1 (WS): Work to M, turn work (on first WS row, place all sts after M onto scrap yarn or st holder).
Row 2 (RS): SSK, work to end. 1 st dec.
Rep Rows 1-2 once more, then work one more WS row.
Last Row (RS): Sl1, K2tog 17 (18, 21, 22, 24)(25, 27, 28, 30) times, K1, break yarn. 19 (20, 23, 24, 26)(27, 29, 30, 32) sts.

Back

Join new ball of yarn at right back.
Row 1 (RS): K1, work 88 (92, 108, 116, 128)(136, 148, 156, 168) sts as established, K1, place the following 14 (16, 16, 20, 20)(26, 26, 30, 30) sts onto scrap yarn or st holder, turn work.

Work back sts as established, slipping the first st and knitting the last st of every row, for 61 (63, 67, 69, 73)(75, 79, 81, 85) rows.

Final Back Row (RS): Sl1, K2tog 17 (18, 21, 22, 24)(25, 27, 28, 30) times, K1, PM, K18 (18, 22, 26, 30)(34, 38, 42, 46), PM, K1, K2tog 17 (18, 21, 22, 24)(25, 27, 28, 30) times, K1, break yarn. 56 (58, 68, 74, 82)(88, 96, 102, 110) sts.

Left Front
Setup Row (RS): Join new ball of yarn at right edge of left front; K1, work to end as established.
Work left front sts as established for 37 (39, 43, 45, 49)(51, 55, 57, 61) more rows, knitting the last st of every WS row and slipping the first st of every RS row.

Neck Shaping
Setup Row (RS): Work to last 12 (12, 14, 16, 18)(20, 22, 24, 26) sts, K2tog, place the last 10 (10, 12, 14, 16)(18, 20, 22, 24) sts onto scrap yarn or st holder. 38 (40, 46, 48, 52)(54, 58, 60, 64) sts.
Row 1 (WS): Sl1, work as established to end.
Row 2 (RS): Sl1, work as established to last 2 sts, K2tog. 1 st dec.
Rep Rows 1-2 once more, then work one more WS row.
Last Row (RS): Sl1, K2tog 17 (18, 21, 22, 24)(25, 27, 28, 30) times, K1, break yarn. 19 (20, 23, 24, 26)(27, 29, 30, 32) sts.

Left Saddle Shoulder
Saddle is worked from top at neck down to outside of shoulder.
Place left shoulder sts on needle as follows: Starting at front left neck edge, place 19 (20, 23, 24, 26)(27, 29, 30, 32) left shoulder sts onto needle, then starting at shoulder edge, place 19 (20, 23, 24, 26)(27, 29, 30, 32) left back shoulder sts onto needle, ending at M.
On larger separate needle or DPN, CO 26 sts using a Provisional Cast On method.
Setup Row (working into provisional CO sts): P1, PM, K2, work Sleeve Chevron Braided Cable Chart over 20 sts, K2, PM, P1, turn work.
Row 1 (RS): Sl1, SM, P2, work Sleeve Chevron Braided Cable Chart over 20 sts, P2, SM, SSK (working last saddle st tog with a back shoulder st), turn work.
Row 2 (WS): Sl1, SM, K2, work Sleeve Chevron Braided Cable Chart over 20 sts, K2, SM, P2tog (working last saddle st tog with a front shoulder st), turn work.
Rep Rows 1-2 until all shoulder sts are used up, ending with a WS row. 26 sts.

Left Sleeve
Setup Rnd (RS): Sl1, SM (this M is BOR M), P2, work Sleeve Chevron Braided Cable Chart as established over 20 sts, P2, SM, K1, PU and K 31 (32, 34, 35, 37)(38, 40, 41, 43) sts from back armhole, work 14 (16, 16, 20, 20)(26, 26, 30, 30) held underarm sts in Moss Stitch, PU and K 19 (20, 22, 23, 25)(26, 28, 29, 31) sts from front armhole, K1, SM. 90 (94, 98, 104, 108)(116, 120, 126, 130) sts.
Rnd 1: P2, work Sleeve Chevron Braided Cable Chart over 20 sts, P2, SM, K1, work Moss Stitch to last st, K1.
Dec Rnd: P2, work Sleeve Chevron Braided Cable Chart over 20 sts, P2, SM, SSK, work Moss Stitch to last 2 sts, K2tog. 2 sts dec.
Cont as established and rep Dec Rnd every six rnds 20 (19, 21, 21, 23)(24, 23, 26, 25) more times. 48 (54, 54, 60, 60)(66, 72, 72, 78) sts.
Cont as established without decs until sleeve measures 20 (20.25, 20.75, 21.25, 21.5)(22, 22.5, 23, 23.5)" from pickup, or 2 (2, 2.25, 2.25, 2.5)(2.5, 2.5, 2.5, 2.5)" shorter than desired length.
Switch to smaller needles and work 3x3 Rib for 2 (2, 2.25, 2.25, 2.5)(2.5, 2.5, 2.5, 2.5)".
BO in pattern.

Right Saddle Shoulder
Place right shoulder sts on needle as follows: Starting at front right neck edge, place 19 (20, 23, 24, 26)(27, 29, 30, 32) right shoulder sts onto needle, then continuing at shoulder edge, place 19 (20, 23, 24, 26)(27, 29, 30, 32) right back shoulder sts onto needle, ending at M.
On larger separate needle or DPN, CO 26 sts using a Provisional Cast On method.
Setup Row: P1, PM, K2, work Sleeve Chevron Braided Cable Chart over 20 sts, K2, PM, P1, turn work.
Row 1 (RS): Sl1, SM, P2, work Sleeve Chevron Braided Cable Chart over 20 sts, P2, SM, SSK (working last saddle st tog with a front shoulder st), turn work. 1 st dec.
Row 2 (WS): Sl1, SM, K2, work Sleeve Chevron Braided Cable Chart over 20 sts, K2, SM, P2tog (working last saddle st tog with a back shoulder st), turn work. 1 st dec.
Rep Rows 1-2 until all shoulder sts are used up, ending with a WS row. 26 sts.

Right Sleeve
Setup Rnd: (RS) Sl1, SM (this M is BOR M), P2, work Sleeve Chevron Braided Cable Chart over 20 sts, P2, SM, K1, PU and K 19 (20, 22, 23, 25)(26, 28, 29, 31) sts from front armhole, work 14 (16, 16, 20, 20)(26, 26, 30, 30) underarm sts in Moss Stitch, PU and K 31 (32, 34, 35, 37)(38, 40, 41, 43) sts from back armhole, K1, SM. 90 (94, 98, 104, 108)(116, 120, 126, 130) sts.
Rnd 1: P2, work Sleeve Chevron Braided Cable Chart over 20 sts, P2, SM, K1, work Moss Stitch to last st, K1.
Dec Rnd: P2, work Sleeve Chevron Braided Cable Chart for 20 sts, P2, SM, SSK, work Moss st to last 2 sts, K2tog. 2 sts dec.
Cont as established and rep Dec Rnd every six rnds 20 (19, 21, 21, 23)(24, 23, 26, 25) more times. 48 (54, 54, 60, 60)(66, 72, 72, 78) sts.
Cont as established without decs until sleeve measures 20 (20.25, 20.75, 21.25, 21.5)(22, 22.5, 23, 23.5)" from pickup, or 2 (2, 2.25, 2.25, 2.5)(2.5, 2.5, 2.5, 2.5)" shorter than desired length.
Switch to smaller needles and work 3x3 Rib for 2 (2, 2.25, 2.25, 2.5)(2.5, 2.5, 2.5, 2.5)".
BO in pattern.

Collar
With smaller needles and starting at right front, K the 10 (10, 12, 14, 16)(18, 20, 22, 24) held sts, PU and K 6 sts from right front, K26 sts from right saddle, K18 (18, 22, 26, 30)(34, 38, 42, 46) sts across back neck, K26 sts from left saddle, PU and K 6 sts from left front, K 6 (6, 8, 10, 12)(14, 16, 18, 20) sts from left front, Sl4. 102 (102, 110, 118, 126)(134, 142, 150, 158) sts total.

Setup Row (WS): *P51 (51, 28, 20, 63)(34, 24, 75, 40), P2tog; rep from * 0 (0, 2, 4, 0)(2, 4, 0, 2) more times, P to last 4 sts, Sl4. 1 (1, 3, 5, 1)(3, 5, 1, 3) sts dec. 101 (101, 107, 113, 125)(131, 137, 149, 155) sts total.

Row 1 (RS): K4, (P3, K3) to last 7 sts, P3, Sl4.

Row 2 (WS): P4, (K3, P3) to last 7 sts, K3, Sl4.

Cont ribbing as established until collar reaches 1.75".

Collar-Turn Row (RS): K4, P to last 4 sts, Sl4.

Row 1 (WS): P2tog, P2, (P3, K3) to last 7 sts, P4, SSP, P1. 99 (99, 105, 111, 123)(129, 135, 147, 153) sts.

Row 2 (RS): Sl1, SSK, (K3, P3) to last 6 sts, K3, K2tog, K1. 97 (97, 103, 109, 121)(127, 133, 145, 151) sts.

Row 3: Sl1, P2tog, P2, K3, (P3, K3) to last 5 sts, P2, SSP, P1. 95 (95, 101, 107, 119)(125, 131, 143, 149) sts.

Row 4: Sl1, (K3, P3) to last 4 sts, K4.

Row 5: Sl1, (P3, K3) to last 4 sts, P4.

Rep Rows 4–5 until collar measures 3.5".

BO in pattern.
Sew BO edge to inside of collar.

Finishing
Weave in all ends, wash, and block to measurements. Measure fronts and order appropriate size zipper. Sew zipper in. (Zipper lengths are approx 22 (23, 24.5, 25.5, 26.25)(27.5, 28.5, 29, 29.5)".)

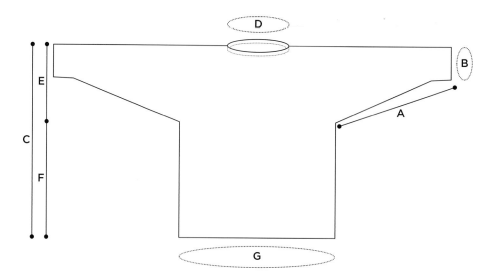

A   *sleeve length* 20 (20.5, 20.75, 21.25, 21.5)(22, 22.5, 23, 23.5)"
B   *cuff circumference* 8 (9, 9, 10, 10)(11, 12, 12, 13)"
C   *total length* 27.25(28.75, 30.25, 31.5, 32.6)(34, 35, 35.75, 36.25)"
D   *neck circumference* 15 (16, 17, 19, 20)(21, 23, 24, 25)"
E   *armhole depth* 10.25 (10.7, 11.25, 12, 12.5)(13.5, 14, 14.75, 15.25)"
F   *body length* 17 (18, 19, 19.5, 20)(20.5, 21, 21, 21)"
G   *chest circumference* 34 (38, 42, 46, 50)(54, 58, 62, 66)"

LEGEND

☐ **K**
RS: Knit stitch
WS: Purl stitch

⊡ **P**
RS: Purl stitch
WS: Knit stitch

2 over 1 Right Cable (2/1 RC)
Sl1 to CN, hold in back; K2, K1 from CN

2 over 1 Left Cable (2/1 LC)
Sl2 to CN, hold in front; K1, K2 from CN

2 over 1 Right Cable, Purl back (2/1 RPC)
Sl1 to CN, hold in back; K2, P1 from CN

2 over 1 Left Cable, Purl back (2/1 LPC)
Sl2 to CN, hold in front; P1, K2 from CN

2 over 2 Right Cable (2/2 RC)
Sl2 to CN, hold in back; K2, K2 from CN

2 over 2 Left Cable (2/2 LC)
Sl2 to CN, hold in front; K2, K2 from CN

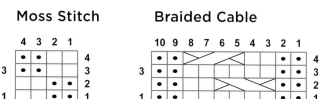

Moss Stitch   Braided Cable

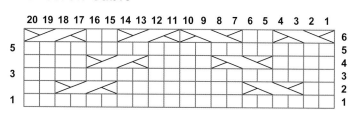

Chevron Cable

Diamond Chart 1
34 (-, -, -, -)(-, -, -, -)" size

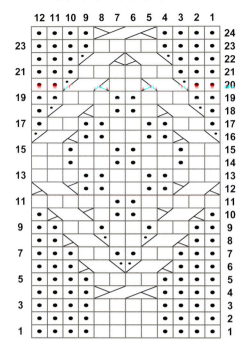

Diamond Chart 2
- (38, 42, -, 50)(-, 58, -, 66)" sizes

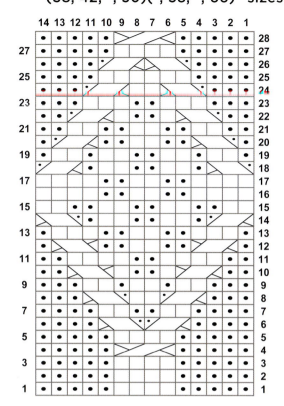

Diamond Chart 3
- (-, -, 46, -)(54, -, 62, -)" sizes

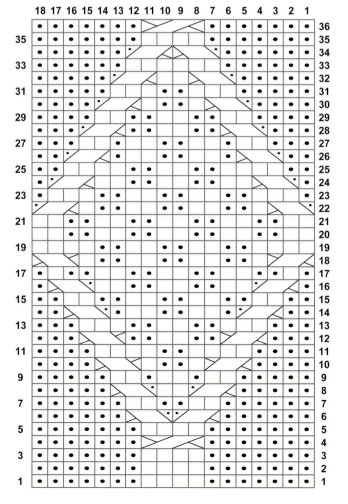

Sleeve Chevron

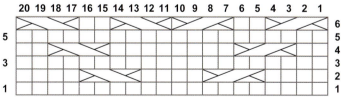

Emre Pullover & Cardigan

Glossary
Common Stitches & Techniques

Slipped Stitches (Sl)
Always slip stitches purl-wise with yarn held to the wrong side of work, unless noted otherwise in the pattern.

Make 1 Left-Leaning Stitch (M1L)
Inserting LH needle from front to back, PU the horizontal strand between the st just worked and the next st, and K TBL.

Make 1 Right-Leaning Stitch (M1R)
Inserting LH needle from back to front, PU the horizontal strand between the st just worked and the next st, and K TFL.

Slip, Slip, Knit (SSK)
(Sl1 K-wise) twice; insert LH needle into front of these 2 sts and knit them together.

Centered Double Decrease (CDD)
Slip first and second sts together as if to work K2tog; K1; pass 2 slipped sts over the knit st.

Stockinette Stitch (St st, flat over any number of sts)
Row 1 (RS): Knit all sts.
Row 2 (WS): Purl all sts.
Rep Rows 1-2 for pattern.
St st in the round: Knit every rnd.
Rev St st is the opposite—purl on RS, knit on WS.

Garter Stitch (in the round over any number of sts)
Rnd 1: Purl all sts.
Rnd 2: Knit all sts.
Rep Rnds 1-2 for pattern.
Garter Stitch flat: Knit every row.
(One Garter *ridge* is comprised of two rows/rnds.)

1x1 Rib (flat or in the round, over an even number of sts)
Row/Rnd 1: (K1, P1) to end of row/rnd.
Rep Row/Rnd 1 for pattern.

2x2 Rib (flat over a multiple of 4 sts plus 2)
Row 1 (RS): K2, (P2, K2) to end of row.
Row 2 (WS): P2, (K2, P2) to end of row.
Rep Rows 1-2 for pattern.

2x2 Rib (in the round over a multiple of 4 sts)
Rnd 1: (K2, P2) to end of rnd.
Rep Rnd 1 for pattern.

Knitting in the Round
The Magic Loop technique uses one long circular needle to knit around a small circumference. The Two Circulars technique uses two long circular needles to knit around a small circumference. Photo and video tutorials for these, plus using DPNs and 16" circular needles, can be found at knitpicks.com/learning-center/knitting-in-round.

Backwards Loop Cast On
A simple, all-purpose cast on that can be worked mid-row. Also called Loop or Single Cast On. A tutorial can be found at knitpicks.com/learning-center/backwards-loop-cast-on.

Long Tail Cast On
Fast and neat once you get the hang of it. Also referred to as the Slingshot Cast On. A tutorial can be found at knitpicks.com/learning-center/learn-to-knit.

Cable Cast On
A strong and nice looking basic cast on that can be worked mid-project. A tutorial can be found at tutorials.knitpicks.com/cabled-cast-on.

Knitted Cast On
A basic cast on that can be worked mid-project. A tutorial can be found at knitpicks.com/learning-center/knitted-cast-on.

3-Needle Bind Off
Used to easily seam two rows of live stitches together. A tutorial can be found at knitpicks.com/learning-center/3-needle-bind-off.

Abbreviations

approx	approximately	KFB *(inc 1)*	knit into front and back of stitch	PSSO *(dec 1)*	pass slipped stitch over	SSP *(dec 1)*	slip, slip, purl these 2 stitches together through back loop
BO	bind off	K-wise	knit-wise	PU	pick up		
BOR	beginning of round	LH	left hand	P-wise	purl-wise	SSSK *(dec 2)*	slip, slip, slip, knit these 3 stitches together (like SSK)
CN	cable needle	M	marker	rep	repeat		
C (1, 2…)	color (1, 2…)	M1	make 1 stitch (work same as M1L)	Rev St st	reverse stockinette stitch *(see above)*		
CC	contrast color					St st	stockinette stitch *(see above)*
CDD *(dec 2)*	centered double decrease *(see above)*	M1L *(inc 1)*	make 1 left-leaning stitch *(see above)*	RH	right hand	st(s)	stitch(es)
				rnd(s)	round(s)	TBL	through back loop
CO	cast on	M1R *(inc 1)*	make 1 right-leaning stitch *(see above)*	RS	right side	TFL	through front loop
cont	continue			Sk	skip	tog	together
dec(s)	decrease(es)	MC	main color	SK2P *(dec 2)*	slip K-wise, knit 2 together, pass slipped stitch over	W&T	wrap & turn *(see next page)*
DPN(s)	double pointed needle(s)	P	purl				
		P2tog *(dec 1)*	purl 2 stitches together	SKP *(dec 1)*	slip K-wise, knit, pass slipped stitch over	WE	work even
inc(s)	increase(s)					WS	wrong side
K	knit	P3tog *(dec 2)*	purl 3 stitches together	Sl	slip *(see above)*	WYIB	with yarn in back
K2tog *(dec 1)*	knit 2 stitches together			SM	slip marker	WYIF	with yarn in front
		PM	place marker	SSK *(dec 1)*	slip, slip, knit these 2 stitches together *(see above)*	YO *(inc 1)*	bring yarn over needle from front up over to back
K3tog *(dec 2)*	knit 3 stitches together	PFB *(inc 1)*	purl into front and back of stitch				

Cables
Tutorials for different kinds of cables, including 1 over 1 and 2 over 2, with and without cable needles, can be found at knitpicks.com/learning-center/guides/cables.

Felted Join (to splice yarn)
One method for joining a new length of yarn to the end of one that is already being used. A tutorial can be found at tutorials.knitpicks.com/felted-join.

Mattress Stitch
A neat, invisible seaming method that uses the bars between the first and second stitches on the edges. A tutorial can be found at tutorials.knitpicks.com/mattress-stitch.

Provisional Cast On (crochet method)
Used to cast on stitches that are also a row of live stitches, so they can be put onto a needle and used later.
DIRECTIONS: Using a crochet hook, make a slip knot, then hold knitting needle in left hand, hook in right. With yarn in back of needle, work a chain st by pulling yarn over needle and through chain st. Move yarn back to behind needle, and rep for the number of sts required. Chain a few more sts off the needle, then break yarn and pull end through last chain. (CO sts may be incorrectly mounted; if so, work into backs of these sts.) To unravel later (when sts need to be picked up), pull chain end out; chain should unravel, leaving live sts. A video tutorial can be found at tutorials.knitpicks.com/crocheted-provisional-cast-on.

Provisional Cast On (crochet chain method)
Same result as the crochet method above, but worked differently, so you may prefer one or the other.
DIRECTIONS: With a crochet hook, use scrap yarn to make a slip knot and chain the number of sts to be cast on, plus a few extra sts. Insert tip of knitting needle into first bump of crochet chain. Wrap project yarn around needle as if to knit, and pull yarn through crochet chain, forming first st. Rep this process until you have cast on the correct number of sts. To unravel later (when sts need to be picked up), pull chain out, leaving live sts. A photo tutorial can be found at tutorials.knitpicks.com/crocheted-provisional-cast-on.

Judy's Magic Cast On
This method creates stitches coming out in opposite directions from a seamless center line, perfect for starting toe-up socks.
DIRECTIONS: Make a slip knot and place loop around one of the two needles; anchor loop counts as first st. Hold needles tog, with needle that yarn is attached to on top. In other hand, hold yarn so tail goes over index finger and yarn attached to ball goes over thumb. Bring tip of bottom needle over strand of yarn on finger (top strand), around and under yarn and back up, making a loop around needle. Pull loop snug. Bring top needle (with slip knot) over yarn tail on thumb (bottom strand), around and under yarn and back up, making a loop around needle. Pull loop snug. Cont casting on sts until desired number is reached; top yarn strand always wraps around bottom needle, and bottom yarn strand always wraps around top needle. A tutorial can be found at tutorials.knitpicks.com/judys-magic-cast-on.

Stretchy Bind Off
DIRECTIONS: K2, *insert LH needle into front of 2 sts on RH needle and knit them tog—1 st remains on RH needle. K1; rep from * until all sts have been bound off. A tutorial can be found at tutorials.knitpicks.com/go-your-own-way-socks-toe-up-part-7-binding-off.

Jeny's Surprisingly Stretchy Bind Off (for 1x1 Rib)
DIRECTIONS: Reverse YO, K1, pass YO over; *YO, P1, pass YO and previous st over P1; reverse YO, K1, pass YO and previous st over K1; rep from * until 1 st is left, then break working yarn and pull it through final st to complete BO.

Kitchener Stitch (also called Grafting)
Seamlessly join two sets of live stitches together.
DIRECTIONS: With an equal number of sts on two needles, break yarn leaving a tail approx four times as long as the row of sts, and thread through a blunt yarn needle. Hold needles parallel with WSs facing in and both needles pointing to the right. Perform Step 2 on the first front st, then Step 4 on the first back st, then continue from Step 1, always pulling yarn tightly so the grafted row tension matches the knitted fabric:
Step 1: Pull yarn needle K-wise through front st and drop st from knitting needle.
Step 2: Pull yarn needle P-wise through next front st, leaving st on knitting needle.
Step 3: Pull yarn needle P-wise through first back st and drop st from knitting needle.
Step 4: Pull yarn needle K-wise through next back st, leaving st on knitting needle.
Rep Steps 1–4 until all sts have been grafted together, finishing by working Step 1 through the last remaining front st, then Step 3 through the last remaining back st. Photo tutorials can be found at knitpicks.com/learning-center/learn-to-knit/kitchener.

Short Rows
There are several options for how to handle short rows, so you may see different suggestions/intructions in a pattern.

Wrap and Turn (W&T) (one option for Short Rows)
Work until the st to be wrapped. If knitting: Bring yarn to front, Sl next st P-wise, return yarn to back; turn work, and Sl wrapped st onto RH needle. Cont across row. If purling: Bring yarn to back of work, Sl next st P-wise, return yarn to front; turn work and Sl wrapped st onto RH needle. Cont across row. **Picking up Wraps:** Work to wrapped st. If knitting: Insert RH needle under wrap, then through wrapped st K-wise; K st and wrap tog. If purling: Sl wrapped st P-wise onto RH needle, use LH needle to lift wrap and place it onto RH needle; Sl wrap and st back onto LH needle, and P tog. A tutorial for W&T can be found at tutorials.knitpicks.com/short-rows-wrap-and-turn-or-wt.

German Short Rows (another option for Short Rows)
Work to turning point; turn. WYIF, Sl first st P-wise. Bring yarn over back of right needle, pulling firmly to create a "double stitch" on RH needle. If next st is a K st, leave yarn at back; if next st is a P st, bring yarn to front between needles. When it's time to work into double st, knit both strands tog. A video tutorial for German Short Rows can be found at knitpicks.com/video/german-short-rows.

Glossary

THIS COLLECTION FEATURES

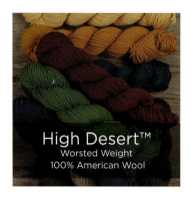

High Desert™
Worsted Weight
100% American Wool

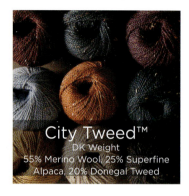

City Tweed™
DK Weight
55% Merino Wool, 25% Superfine Alpaca, 20% Donegal Tweed

Simply Wool™
Bulky Weight
100% Eco Wool

Stroll™
Fingering Weight
75% Fine Superwash Merino Wool, 25% Nylon

Swish™
DK & Bulky Weights
100% Fine Superwash Merino Wool

Twill™
Worsted Weight
100% Superwash Merino Wool

Woodland Tweed™ Bare
Aran/Heavy Worsted Weight
80% Merino Wool, 15% Baby Alpaca, 5% Viscose

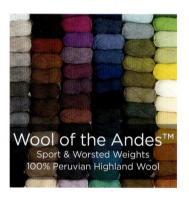

Wool of the Andes™
Sport & Worsted Weights
100% Peruvian Highland Wool

Wool of the Andes™ Tweed
Worsted Weight
80% Peruvian Highland Wool, 20% Donegal Tweed

View these beautiful yarns and more at www.KnitPicks.com

Knit Picks®

Knit Picks yarn is both luxe and affordable—a seeming contradiction trounced! But it's not just about the pretty colors; we also care deeply about fiber quality and fair labor practices, leaving you with a gorgeously reliable product you'll turn to time and time again.